WORLD SERIES
THRILLS

WORLD SERIES THRILLS

by Stu Black

Watermill Press

ISBN 0-89375-824-8

Cover photo: Mickey Palmer/Focus on Sports

Photos on pages 3, 8—Courtesy National Baseball Hall of Fame and Museum, Cooperstown, New York; photos on pages 16, 27, 33, 38, 45, 48, 58, 67, 76, 89, 94, 101—Wide World Photos

CONTENTS

BILL WAMBSGANSS'
UNASSISTED TRIPLE PLAY—1920

The 1920 World Series was played under two clouds.
The first cloud formed because the 1919 Series had
been fixed. Eight days before the battle for the 1920
championship began, a grand jury in Cook County,
Illinois accused eight Chicago White Sox players of
conspiring to throw the 1919 Series.

The second cloud appeared late in the 1920 season.
On August 16, Cleveland shortstop Ray Chapman
was hit in the head by a pitch thrown by the New York
Yankees' Carl Mays. Chapman died in a hospital the
next day.

It was strange that baseball was suddenly operating
out of a hole. The sport had made a strong comeback at
the close of World War I. The interest in the 1919
Series, Chicago White Sox versus the Cincinnati Reds,
had been so intense, that it was decided to increase the
number of games. That year, the Series became a five-
out-of-nine event, instead of four of seven.

The 1920 Series pitted the Cleveland Indians against
the Brooklyn Dodgers. The Brooklyn club had been
called ''The Dodgers'', short for Trolley Dodgers,

since before the turn of the century. (Brooklyn residents were generally called Trolley Dodgers since the streets had been made hazardous by the newfangled trolley cars.) These days, however, it was not unusual to hear them referred to as "The Robins," after their manager, the legendary Wilbert Robinson.

On the field, the Robins were led by Hall-of-Fame left fielder Zack Wheat, center fielder Hy Myers, and Hall-of-Fame pitcher Burleigh Grimes. Wheat hit .328 in 1920, the fourth best mark in the National League. Myers also topped the .300 mark (.304) and knocked in 80 runs, the league's fifth best total. Grimes won 23 games and was among the league leaders in every important pitching category. The Boys from Flatbush grabbed the lead early in the season, then held off a late charge by their cross-town rivals, the Manhattan-based New York Giants. It was their second pennant in five years.

The Indians, in winning their first pennant ever, were managed by all-time great Tris Speaker. Speaker, then a 12-year veteran, was a player-manager who led his team by example. His best example was the .388 batting average he had compiled that year. He also played center field the way it was supposed to be played.

Cleveland was the sentimental favorite to win this Series. Following Ray Chapman's death, the Indians launched a spirited drive that dethroned the defending-champion White Sox and held off the Yankees.

It has been said that strong pitching won the pennant for Cleveland. The Indians threw a tough pitcher at the opposition every day. Jim Bagby was 31–12, Hall-of-

Cleveland's power-hitter, Elmer Smith. (1920)

Famer Stanley Coveleski was 24–14, Ray Caldwell was 20–10, and former Dodger Walter "Duster" Mails, brought up from the minors in August, was 7–0.

Coveleski, the husky, spitball-throwing right-hander from the West Pennsylvania mining country, was the pitching star of the series. His performance was the best seen in interleague competition since the Giants' Christy Mathewson, another Pennsylvanian, pitched three shutouts against the Philadelphia Athletics in the 1905 Series. Coveleski gave up only one hit more than Matty had—15—in defeating Brooklyn three times. He allowed only five hits in each victory. He did yield two runs.

Coveleski got Cleveland off to a good start, beating the Robins 3–1 in the first game. His mound opponent was Hall-of-Famer Rube Marquard. The day's best batsman was Cleveland catcher Steve O'Neill, who banged out two doubles. The Robins got even the next day as Burleigh Grimes spun a seven-hit shutout, 3–0.

The third game, also played in Brooklyn, saw the Robins parlay a 2–1 victory into a 2–1 lead in games. As expected, the pitching was dominating the hitting.

After the third game, there was a one-day lapse to allow the World Series caravan—players, coaches, managers, officials, and reporters—to travel to the shores of Lake Erie. In the fourth game, the first one played at Cleveland's League Park, Coveleski repeated his opening-day triumph, winning 5–1. Thus, with the Series all even at two games each, the scene was set for Game Five and one of the great World Series thrills of all time.

The pitching match up for Game Five was a repeat of Game Two. It was Cleveland's Bagby against Brooklyn's Grimes. Once again, each manager sent his best pitcher—the best in each league that season—into action. The home team's Bagby, who had copped 31 victories during the season but had lost Game Two, assured one and all he would even his ledger this day. A tough spitball pitcher, Grimes was a special favorite of manager Robinson. A tenacious competitor, Grimes had pitched a shutout in Game Two. This day, however, he couldn't even pitch a shutout through the first inning.

After the Robins went down without scoring in the first, Cleveland left fielder Charley Jamieson led off with a single off first baseman Ed Konetchy's glove. Actually, Konetchy made a good play getting to the ball. His quick movements kept the ball from going down the line for a double.

With Jamieson jumping off first base, repeatedly faking as if he were going to try to steal second, Grimes pitched to second baseman Bill Wambsganss. Numerous throws over to first failed to pick Jamieson off, though it did cut down on his lead. Finally, Grimes came in to the patient Wambsganss, who promptly lined the ball into left field. The ball was hit so hard that, even though Jamieson was running on the pitch, he had to stop at second base. The next batter, Tris Speaker, bunted, and when Grimes fell down trying to field his squibbler, the bases were full. The next batter was right fielder Elmer Smith. Smith was Cleveland's most powerful hitter. He had hit 12 homers during the season,

5

which was good enough for fifth best in the American League. The count was one ball and two strikes when Smith caught hold of a high, sharp, breaking spitball and drove it way behind the right-field fence. When the Indian merry-go-round had stopped, four runs had scored. Cleveland was jubilant. It was the first grand-slam homer in World Series history. It was also the first "first" of the day.

Indian first baseman Doc Johnson opened the fourth frame by singling off Grimes' shin. Grimes may have been a great pitcher, but, on this day at least, his fielding was second rate. He had failed to handle Speaker's bunt in the first, and that set up the Indians' big inning. Now he was setting up new trouble.

Johnson took second on a passed ball and went to third on an infield out. Catcher Steve O'Neill was then walked intentionally to get at pitcher Jim Bagby. Brooklyn's manager Wilbert Robinson's strategy backfired, however, when Bagby found a delivery he liked and smashed the ball over the right-field barrier for a three-run homer, Cleveland's second four-bagger of the day.

Bagby's homer put two more firsts on the record. His shot was the first round tripper ever hit in the fall classic by a pitcher. It was also the first time a team had scored its first seven runs in a World Series contest strictly by homers.

When Brooklyn came to bat in the top of the fifth, the game was just about out of their reach. They had to make a move now or a 3-2 deficit in games loomed. They knew Bagby was hittable. The Robins had been getting men on base against him in every inning.

6

But they were leaving them there. The trick was to string a few hits back to back. In the fifth inning, Brooklyn got the first two men on base and seemed ready to put the pressure on.

Second baseman Pete Kilduff led off the inning with a single. The 26,884 Cleveland fans, sure that victory was theirs today, continued to whoop it up. However, when catcher Otto Miller followed Kilduff with a single, the ballpark suddenly grew quiet.

The pitcher was due up next for Brooklyn. Clarence Mitchell, who had replaced Grimes on the mound in the fourth, took his position in the batter's box. Mitchell, who had first appeared in a major-league box score in 1911, drove a savage line drive high and to the left of second base. Clearly, it was too high for the six-foot-tall Bagby, who jumped to try and catch it anyway. With the prospect of a third straight hit and a major enemy rally under way, the Cleveland fans held their breath. Fortunately, second baseman Bill Wambsganss was ready. Moving swiftly to his right, he leaped at the last instant and came down clutching the ball in his gloved hand. He hesitated after he landed, looking around for both of the base runners, then moved easily, as if the play in front of him were nothing more than a routine force out. Suddenly, he seemed to realize the golden opportunity that confronted him. Before the startled customers could grasp the play, he sprinted to second and stepped on the bag. At that moment, Pete Kilduff, who had been on second base, was sliding into third, unaware that he had just become the second out.

Bill Wambsganss pulls off an unassisted triple play. (1920)

The moment Otto Miller, who was taking a short lead off first base, heard the bat hit the ball, he was sure it was a base hit. Head down, he came tearing down the base line toward the keystone sack. When he finally looked up, Bill Wambsganss was standing in front of him, a funny grin on his face. Wambsganss applied the tag and began to laugh. Miller was the third out. It was an unassisted triple play, the first and only one of its kind in World Series history. It was one of the most thrilling plays ever made in a World Series game.

The "firsts" did the Robins in. The first grand slam, the first homer by a pitcher, the first unassisted triple play were just too much to overcome. The jig was up now and no one knew it better than the Robins' players.

The Indians went on to win the Series, five games to two. The Robins were so demoralized by the events of the fifth game that they were shut out in the last two contests. This was the second time a Brooklyn team lost a World Series. For the next 35 years, Brooklyn remained the patsy team in the October extravaganza. It wasn't until 1955 that Brooklyn fans were able to hold their heads high.

BABE RUTH
CALLS HIS SHOTS—1932

By the time the 1932 World Series rolled around, Babe Ruth had been major-league baseball's "Sultan Of Swat" for more than a decade. The Babe deserved a royal title because, for all intents and purposes, his regal presence saved baseball. Ruth became the most important player in his sport in 1919, the same year eight members of the Chicago White Sox accepted bribe money to throw the World Series. They were labeled "The Black Sox" when word of their deed became public knowledge. A great outcry arose against professional baseball. Angry fans wondered if they could ever trust what they saw on the diamond again.

That same year, in a separate action, Babe Ruth was sold by the poverty-stricken Boston Red Sox to the rich New York Yankees for $100,000 and a $350,000 loan. In 1919, his last year in Boston, Ruth had hit 29 homers. When he hit 54 as a Yankee in 1920, people were overwhelmed by his feat. He was headline news all over the country. Babe's home-run hitting ability and his show-business personality began to push the Black Sox off the front pages. Soon baseball itself and not the scandal was the focus again.

In addition to his hitting prowess, Ruth was quite a pitcher. He had started his baseball career as a pitcher. His major-league pitching record was 94-46. Twice, he won more than 20 games in a season. In the 1916 and 1918 World Series, he threw 29 ⅔ consecutive scoreless innings, a record that lasted 43 years. After he retired, Ruth often said the World Series scoreless streak was his most prized accomplishment. But the Yankees were buying Ruth's bat, not his arm.

Babe Ruth hit 59 home runs in 1921. He became a national treasure. He had captured the imagination of the American public. Young boys dreamed of growing up to be either President of the United States or Babe Ruth.

Ruth was a larger-than-life character. A great ballplayer, a clutch performer, a magnetic personality, he saved his greatest trick for the last World Series in which he appeared.

It had been four years since the Yankees had been the World Champions. The magnificent Philadelphia Athletics of 1929–1931 had won the American League flag three years running. In 1932, however, another Yankees' squad, again led by the hitting of Ruth and first baseman Lou Gehrig, overpowered all league opposition and stood ready for interleague competition.

The Chicago Cubs were the National League's best that year. They were a good team led by Hall-of-Fame catcher Gabby Harnett and slugging outfielder Kiki Cuyler. While the Cubs' regular line-up was a cut below New York's in talent, the Chicago boys were capable of winning the Series because of their pitching. Hurlers like Hall-of-Famer Burleigh Grimes, who won 270 games in his career, Charlie Root, who put 201 notches in his victory column, Lon Warneke, with a lifetime victory total of 192, and Guy Bush, who brought up the rear with 176 wins, were usually good enough to shut any attack down. The Yankees were not just any attack. That week, each pitcher was thoroughly beaten. Charlie Root was doubly insulted. The man voted the greatest right-handed pitcher in Cub history was not only beaten in the game he pitched, he was a victim of Ruth's showmanship, the patsy in one of the most thrilling moments in baseball history.

The Yankees easily defeated the Cubs in the initial game of the 1932 Series, 12–6. The game was played at Yankee Stadium in the Bronx, "The House That Ruth Built," and the New Yorkers seemed to be able to score at will. Neither starter Guy Bush nor reliever Burleigh Grimes was any kind of mystery to them. The stories that appeared in the next day's papers were about how effective Yankee pitcher Red Ruffing had been, Gehrig's homer and single, and New York's total dominance. There was an underlying story building, however, that went unreported, but led to the 1932 Series being a memorable one.

Bench jockeying in baseball can be vicious. The men in the dugout feel they have a license to say what-ever they want about the opposition. They often shout the worst things that come to mind about each other. The insults are designed to distract the other side from concentrating on the game. It is just another weapon, the players feel, in the never-ending struggle to get the edge. Usually, the insults are without a focus. A stream of words are said about a player's home, looks, family—you name it. This time, the give-and-take between the two opposing dugouts did have a central theme.

Cub shortstop Mark Koenig had played that position for New York for most of the latter half of the 1920s. In 1930, he was sold to the Detroit Tigers. In April of 1932, the Tigers got rid of him, Koenig returning to the minors where he played for the San Francisco Missions of the Pacific Coast League. In August of that year, the Chicago Cub brain trust, spying an infield weakness, decided that a veteran shortstop was needed to help them in their pennant push. They bought Koenig's contract from the Missions on August 5. Koenig played in 33 contests as a Cub, hit .353, and was instrumental in the closing drive that enabled Chicago to beat Pittsburgh. Cub players, however, were not very generous to Koenig when they voted the way the World Series money would be split before the Series began. When Koenig's ex-teammates on the Yankees heard of the small share their friend had been awarded, they were furious. Headed by Babe Ruth, they accused the Cubs of being cheapskates every chance they could. The Cubs answered in kind. The yelling, screaming, insulting, and howling that went on between the dugouts made it seem likely a brawl would break out at any time. Though the teams never came to blows, the bickering never stopped.

With the war of words continuing uninterrupted, the Yankees won the second game. Behind the nine-hit pitching of Lefty Gomez, they beat Chicago 5–2. Again Lou Gehrig was the big Yankee hitter, banging out three hits, knocking in a run. For the second day in a row, Ruth was one for three, a single. While the score was closer than the day before, the contest never really was in doubt.

The Series moved to Chicago for the third game. With the change of cities, the Cub fans took hope. New York had won both games played on their turf, they thought. Now the Cubs could return the favor. If they could win all three games played at Wrigley Field, then they would be within one of winning the World Championship when the Series resumed in New York. They'd only have to win one of the two games played there to capture the crown.

The Yankees quickly showed them their hopes were empty. They shocked the 49,986 spectators with a display of their awesome power. On this day, the New York attack was working full blast. Both Ruth and Gehrig were at the top of their form. Three batters into the game, the Bronx Bombers led 3–0. Cub shortstop Billy Jurges, playing in place of Koenig, allowed New York leadoff man Earle Combs to reach second on his throwing error. The next batter, third baseman Joe Sewell, walked. Babe Ruth then spanked a Charlie Root pitch into the right-field temporary bleachers for three runs. The crowd, which had been noisy and expectant, became quiet.

But the quiet didn't last very long. In the last half of the first, the Cubs scored once, getting the crowd going again. They aimed most of their fury at Ruth. In the second inning, when right fielder Kiki Cuyler caught the Bambino's long bid for his second homer of the day, the crowd went wild. Even though Gehrig led off the third inning with a homer, stretching the New York lead to 4-1, the crowd remained noisy. When the Cubs scored two runs in their half of the third and another in the fourth to tie the game, the crowd noise reached unbearable levels.

Then, in the top of the fifth, a most memorable and controversial event took place. Ruth was the leadoff hitter that inning. Cub fans, bold and happy since their Cubs had caught the mighty Yankees, let Ruth know what they thought of him, his team, and his town. When Charlie Root got the first pitch over for a strike, they repeated everything they had said, and added some new phrases. The Cub bench warmers also joined in the verbal salvo. Looking at the Cub bench, Ruth held up one finger on his right hand, taunting them. *One strike boys,* he seemed to be saying, *that's only one strike.* A second strike brought up the same hand and two outstretched fingers. A ball and he put up one finger on his left hand. A second ball and up went two fingers on his left hand. Then he wiped his hands on his trousers and pointed toward the distant bleachers. Root wound up and threw a fast ball—and Babe hit it out of the park right where he had pointed.

Ever since that ball was swatted, there have been different versions of the facts. Charlie Root and the Cubs claim he was only mocking them, indicating the ball-and-strike count. Most newspapermen who were there, however, side with Joe Sewell's version.

Babe Ruth crosses the plate after calling his home run shot. (1932)

"The Babe was fussing at Burleigh Grimes," Sewell recalls. "Grimes had a towel over his head. I never will forget that. Then Babe backed out of the box, with his bat in his left hand, he was looking at their bench. He never said a word to the pitcher, Root. He was talking to Burleigh Grimes....Then he pointed to the center-field fence with the two fingers on his right hand. Then Babe got back into the box. Root threw a pitch that was just above his knees. I've got a mental picture of the ball going out of the ballpark. It went out in center field, right through a tree. And that tree was loaded with little boys looking at the game. As that ball went through the trees, those boys just vanished; they evaporated. They were all after that ball. No, the Babe was definitely calling his shot."

Ruth's second homer of the game was followed by Gehrig's second homer of the game. The Cubs' resistance was broken. Suddenly, all the talk from their bench eased off. The Yankees had proved their point. They were the better club. The New Yorkers went on to win this game 7-5, then they finished off the job the next day, 13-6. That made 12 consecutive victories for Yankee teams in World Series competition, a record.

That fifth-inning homer by Babe Ruth was his 15th and last in Series play. Appearing in his tenth and final fall classic, Ruth's record of most lifetime Series home runs stood for 32 years, until Mickey Mantle broke it in 1964.

There was one final note about that World Series. Years after that Series was played, every-

MICKEY OWEN'S MISCUE—1941

"The game is never over till it's over," Yogi Berra once said. The Yankee star was never proven more accurate than on a sunny, crisp, autumn afternoon in 1941. On that day, October 5, 1941, Dodger catcher Mickey Owen gained lasting infamy because he failed to catch what would have been a game-ending third strike. Instead of closing out the Dodgers' second triumph of the World Series, Yankee batter Tommy Henrich scurried safely to first. Then New York, only behind 4–3 at the time, pulled out their thunder and lightning attack and beat Brooklyn 7–4. It was the pivotal play in the pivotal game of the Series. Instead of the teams being tied at two games each, New York took a commanding 3–1 lead.

It's unfortunate a mistake like that happens to anyone. Mickey Owen was an excellent defensive catcher. He had originally signed with the St. Louis Cardinal organization and worked his way up through their farm system. In 1937, he graduated to the Cardinals, spending four years in St. Louis. In those four seasons, his top batting average was only .267. Clearly, Owen wasn't in the big leagues because of a great bat. His speciality was defense.

That fact was well understood around the National League. They especially knew about Owen's abilities in Brooklyn, where they hadn't had a good defensive catcher since Al Lopez in 1935. Realizing they had improved in many areas in their drive to become a serious contender, but were still lacking in defense behind the plate, Brooklyn traded for Owen. In December of 1940 the Dodgers gave St. Louis two players and $60,000 in cash for him.

Owen's acquisition proved to be a very wise move. He caught 128 games for the 1941 Dodgers, and he was a key cog in their march to the National League pennant. Between April 15 and August 29 of that year, Owen accepted 476 chances without making an error, a major-league record. The errorless streak lasted exactly 100 games.

Later that year, he set another major-league record when he caught three foul pop-ups in one inning. But few people remember his defensive excellence. All they remember is his telltale miscue.

When the Dodgers played in Brooklyn (they moved to Los Angeles after the 1957 season), their fans uttered a favorite saying at the end of every disappointing season, "Wait till next year." As the 1941 season began, it seemed possible that "next year" had finally arrived.

Larry MacPhail, a tough man with a hot temper, ran the Dodgers in 1941. MacPhail was an innovator, a man who was smart enough and daring enough to try new things. When he ran the Cincinnati franchise in 1935, he had lights installed at the ballpark, and the Reds were the first major-league team to play baseball at night. Baseball at night was a novel idea then. People laughed at MacPhail. Today, people laugh at the Chicago Cubs because they are the only team whose ballpark has no lights.

MacPhail knew how to build teams as well as lighting systems. The Cincinnati team he constructed won pennants in both 1939 and 1940, winning the World Championship in the latter year. By the time the Reds were king of the hill, MacPhail had moved on. He had taken over the Brooklyn club in 1938. When he arrived in Brooklyn, the situation was similar to what it had been in Cincinnati in 1934. Much work had to be done to improve a floundering Dodger ballclub that in 1938 had finished seventh in an eight-team league. Ballplayers were imported by the carload. In 1939, MacPhail hired the fiesty Leo Durocher to manage his team. That year, the Dodgers jumped up four spots, finishing third. The following year, they moved up to second place.

In 1940, MacPhail made a key move when he "stole" young Pee Wee Reese, a classy shortstop, out of the Boston Red Sox farm system. With Dolf Camilli at first base and Harry "Cookie" Lavagetto at third, the pieces were beginning to fall into place. When veteran second baseman Billy Herman was purchased from the Cubs in May of 1941, the infield had the look of a winner.

MacPhail got his hands on a second topnotch young player in 1940 in outfielder Pete Reiser. In 1941, his first full season with Brooklyn, Reiser led the league in batting average (.343), doubles (39), triples (17), runs scored (117), and slugging percentage (.558). In addition, he played an excellent defensive outfield. Reiser was surrounded by Hall-of-Famer Joe Medwick in left field and the popular Dixie Walker in right. The trio formed quite an outfield. The lowest batting average in the Dodgers' outer garden that year was Walker's .311.

Brooklyn's pitching was adequate. MacPhail had bought Kirby Higbe in from Philadelphia to bolster the staff. It turned out to be an inspired move as Higbe won 22 games to tie teammate Whitlow Wyatt for the league high in that category. Third starter Curt Davis won 13 games, and reliever Hugh Casey was superb all season. The Dodgers had good enough pitching to win the pennant by 2½ games.

The Dodgers' 1941 opponents were the New York Yankees. It was the first, but certainly not the last time that the boroughs of Brooklyn and the Bronx went head to head for the number-one position in baseball. If being in the World Series was strange fare to the Dodgers (they hadn't been in a Series since 1920), it was old hat to the Yankees. Led by Hall-of-Fame manager Joe McCarthy, the Bronxites seemed to have a permanent invitation to participate in post-season play. New York had won four straight world Championships between 1936 and 1939. They had lost the American League pennant to Detroit in 1940, but corrected that oversight the following year. When the 1941 season ended, the Yankees were back to their accustomed perch, atop the American League standings. After 154 games, they were 17 games better than second-place Boston. Their lineup included such siege guns as Joe DiMaggio, Tommy Henrich,

Charley Keller, Joe Gordon, and Bill Dickey. In addition, like the Dodgers, they had come up with a small man to play big at shortstop. Phil Rizzuto stabilized the Yankee infield in much the same manner that Pee Wee Reese stabilized the Dodgers.

It had been a strange year for the Yankees. On the minus side, all-time great Lou Gehrig had died in June, a few weeks short of his 38th birthday. Though no longer an active player, his youthful death was keenly felt in the Bronx.

On the plus side was DiMaggio's record-breaking 56-game hitting streak. For two months, the excitement of his streak captured the nation's attention. Only the United States entry into World War II later in the year attracted more press coverage. The streak was a national soap opera. Even people who didn't care about baseball checked to see what Joe had done yesterday. The streak started on May 15 in New York and ended July 17 in Cleveland.

The Yankees went into their 12th World Series confident they would emerge with their ninth World Championship. They were lordly and haughty and considered the World Championship to be their property. To them, Cincinnati's victory in 1940 was a hoax, a case of someone stealing something that belonged to them. They were now prepared to return the championship to where it belonged.

New York broke out on top, winning the first game 3–2. Yankee pitcher Red Ruffing notched his sixth World Series victory in this game, tying him for the most lifetime World Series triumphs by a pitcher up to that time. It was a quiet game, featuring good pitching and the hitting of Yankee second baseman Joe Gordon. Gordon got two hits, including the game's only homer. For the Dodgers, only Reese had a good day. The 23-year-old shortstop had three singles and scored one of the Dodger runs.

Brooklyn bounced back the next day and eked out a 3–2 victory behind the nine-hit pitching of Whitlow Wyatt. That second-game victory put the Dodgers in pretty good shape. They had split the first two games at Yankee Stadium. The next three games would be at home, where they figured to have an advantage. The Dodger clubhouse was boisterous after the second-game triumph.

"We got them now," the Dodgers yelled. "Wait till we get them in Brooklyn. We'll murder the bums."

The players were singing in the showers, throwing wet towels at each other, and generally acting as if they had already cashed the World Series' checks.

The Dodgers were victims of a cruel break in the third game. They had started a hardened veteran, "Fat" Freddy Fitzsimmons, a man with World Series experience. Though his record was only 6–1 in 1941, Fitzsimmons pitched a terrific game shutting out the Yankees through seven innings.

The bad break came in the Yankees' half of the seventh inning. There were two out and Yankee pitcher Marius Russo was at the plate. He smashed a low line drive back at Fitzsimmons. The ball crashed into the pitcher's left knee and popped into the air. It went high enough so the ball was caught on the fly by Reese for the third out. Unfortunately, it crippled Fitzsimmons for the rest of the game and the Series.

He collapsed in a heap, then was helped from the field, limping. In the next inning, with Dodger reliever Hugh Casey pitching, the Yankees struck. Consecutive hits by third baseman Red Rolfe, right fielder Tommy Henrich, center fielder DiMaggio, and left fielder Charley Keller netted two runs, one more than the Dodgers were able to score in their last two times at bat.

For Game Four, the fans streamed into Ebbets Field, muttering against the evil fate that had befallen Fitzsimmons yesterday and cost the Dodgers a game. But today was another day, they reasoned. Win today and the Series was even again.

The Dodgers didn't win on October 5, 1941. In fact it was one of the darkest days in Brooklyn's storied baseball history. Never had victory been torn so rudely from a club's grasp in a World Series game as it was torn from the Dodger's grasp that day.

The starting pitchers were Kirby Higbe, 22-9 for the National League champions during the season, and Atley Donald, 9-5 for New York. The Yankees tapped Higbe for a run in the second and two more in the fourth, forcing his early removal. But the Dodgers put two runs up on the scoreboard in both the fourth and fifth to take a one-run lead. Hugh Casey came in to pitch in the fifth, and this day the man from Georgia was on his game. He held the Yanks scoreless for over three innings and took that one-run lead into the ninth.

The first two batters were easy outs. Casey had but one out to go. The Brooklyn crowd was roaring. One more out and a celebration would begin. The Yankee batter was Tommy Henrich, who later in his career would earn the nickname "Old Reliable" because he was so good in important situations. This time, however, Henrich was overmatched. With the count three balls, two strikes, Casey threw a curveball that exploded across the plate and down. The ball not only exploded past Henrich's bat, but past Mikey Owen's glove also. As the catcher raced to the backstop to retrieve the bouncing ball, Henrich ran to first base. Fans who had taken their eye off the field after Henrich swung and missed were delirious. The game was over, they thought. The last man had struck out. They were dancing in the Ebbets Field aisles. Paper and confetti were thrown into the air. Suddenly, they realized something was terribly wrong. The Dodgers weren't jumping for joy. They weren't even running off the field. DiMaggio was coming up; and the Dodgers were still in defensive positions. The great Yankee center fielder had hit safely in 17 more games after his 56-game streak was stopped. As hard as it was to believe, Number 5 had hit safely in 73 out of 74 games.

DiMaggio wasted little time belting a screaming single to left. Henrich stopped at second. On the mound, Hugh Casey was ripping mad. His emotions were out of control. He should have been coached to slow down and relax, but strangely Leo Durocher never came to the mound to talk to him.

Charley Keller, who already had three hits on the day, was due up. He took two called strikes. With the count 0-2, Casey thought he would outsmart the powerful Yankee left fielder by not wasting a pitch

Mickey Owen fails to catch a third strike and opens the door to a Yankee win. (1941)

and trying to slip the next one over. Keller was ready. He smashed the pitch against the right-field wall. It was a two-run double. The Yankees led 5–4 and a pin could be heard dropping at the Brooklyn ballpark.

The blood-thirsty Yankees could have stopped there, but that wasn't their style. They didn't stop until two more runs crossed the plate. Casey, in a blind rage, walked Dickey, and Gordon doubled to left, scoring both Keller and Dickey. The score was 7–4. Finally, mercifully, after Rizzuto walked, the side was retired.

As if in a trance, the Dodgers went out in their half of the ninth. The Yankees had won, and everybody seemed to know that nothing could save the Dodgers on the morrow.

Nothing did; the Yankees beat them 3–1. It was all over for another year. The Dodgers had expired for 1941 when the ball sailed behind Owen. As the Dodger fans were leaving Ebbets Field that afternoon, more than one was heard to say, "Wait till next year."

COOKIE LAVAGETTO
BREAKS UP BILL BEVANS' BID
FOR A NO-HITTER—1947

World War II was finally over and peace was marvelous. New and wonderful things were happening in baseball. All of the great players had returned, older but unharmed. DiMaggio was back, as were Boston's Ted Williams, and Cleveland's fireballing right hander Bob Feller. So were St. Louis' Stan Musial and Pittsburgh's Hank Greenberg. They were joined in 1946 by a black man named Jackie Robinson.

Brooklyn Dodger vice president Branch Rickey may well have been the smartest man ever associated with the game of baseball. A highly principled man, he thought the ban on blacks in the major leagues was morally wrong. A learned man, he knew the Constitution said that everybody was entitled to equal opportunity. A pragmatic man, he knew it was good business to be the first team to take advantage of the pool of great ballplayers hidden in the Negro leagues.

Jackie Robinson was a great ballplayer. The Brooklyn Dodgers won the pennant in 1947 with the first baseman Robinson capturing the Rookie-of-the-Year award. Gil Hodges, who replaced Robinson at first the following year (Jackie moved to second), and center fielder Duke Snider, also joined the Dodgers that year. Right fielder Carl Furillo had joined the Dodgers the previous year. All had come through the minor-league "farm" system Rickey had constructed. Add Pee Wee Reese, and the club that would dominate the National League for most of the 1950s was taking shape.

Robinson was not the only major story concerning the Brooklyn ballclub in 1947. Rarely has a team had a dizzier year and still won a pennant. Dodger manager Leo Durocher, at the helm since 1939, was suspended for the entire season during spring training. On the eve of the season, Durocher was suddenly gone, and Branch Rickey's old friend, Burt Shotton, who hadn't managed a baseball team in 13 years, took over.

It was the Dodgers great misfortune to have an excellent group of players at the same time the Yankees continued to have great teams. When Ruth and Gehrig wore out, New York's assembly-line farm system produced players like Joe DiMaggio, Tommy Henrich, and Charley Keller. Soon after Hall-of-Fame catcher Bill Dickey retired in 1946, Yogi Berra came on the scene.

It came to be that in 1947 the Dodgers and Yankees got together for the second time in the decade. Over the next decade, the teams would meet four more times in World Series competition. In 1947, the Yankees romped to the pennant. They wound up 12 games ahead of their closest pursuer. The Dodgers had a tougher time, eventually pulling out to a five-length victory. As usual, the Yankees had huge hitting muscles. Led by DiMaggio and Henrich, the team's batting average during the season was a healthy .271, the best in the league. New York also led the league in runs scored and homers.

The Yankees were never a one-dimensional team. They could win games with the glove and arm as well as the bat. Blinded by the team's awesome hitting, people often overlooked their excellent pitching and defense. In 1947, the Yankee pitching staff had the league's lowest earned-run average, 3.39.

The one thing the Yanks of 1947 didn't do well was steal bases. The way they hit, and their idea of how to play the game, left the steal out in the cold. The team stole 27 sacks in 1947. Jackie Robinson himself stole 29 for Brooklyn that year.

The Dodgers' attack was more versatile than the Yankees'. They hit .272, and scored about as many runs as the Yanks, but they did it with a combination of power and speed. Their pitching, however, permitted about a half run more per game than New York, an edge for the Yanks. The 1947 World Series shaped up as a match between two powerful clubs.

The first World Series game ever televised was played at Yankee Stadium on September 30, 1947. The Yankees won that day 5-3, behind Frank "Spec" Shea and Joe Page. It was a strange game, one that gave a hint of things to come in this Series. The Dodger starter was Ralph Branca, and the big right hander, who had compiled a 21–12 record during the season, retired the first 12 batters he faced. In the fifth inning, however, he suddenly lost his control and the Yankees banged him out of the box, scoring five runs.

The New Yorkers doubled their previous day's run total in Game Two, beating Brooklyn 10-3. They quickly overpowered the Dodgers, scoring in six of the first seven innings.

Back in Brooklyn for Game Three, the Dodgers finally got into the Series. They proved they could score more than three runs a game, winning a 9-8 slugfest. Yankee starter Bobo Newsom didn't get out of the second inning, when the Dodgers scored six runs. Brooklyn starter, Joe Hatton, managed to stagger until the fifth, when manager Shotton removed him and brought in Hugh Casey. Making his second appearance of the series, Casey shut down the Yankees the rest of this day. He would appear in all the remaining four games of the 1947 Series. Casey was the winning pitcher in Game Three.

Game Four produced one of the most thrilling moments in World Series history. A capacity crowd of 33,443 fans jammed into Ebbets Field on this Friday afternoon, October 3, 1947. They saw the Dodgers start Henry Taylor and the Yankees, Floyd "Bill" Bevans. Actually, late arrivals never got a glimpse of Taylor. Singles by second baseman George "Snuffy" Stirnweiss and Tommy Henrich, plus Pee Wee Reese's error on Berra's ground ball filled the bases before anyone was out. Taylor walked DiMaggio on four pitches and was immediately replaced by Hal Gregg. The score was 1-0 already, and Shotton wanted to try to keep the Yankees close. Gregg stopped the Yanks by getting first baseman George McQuinn to pop up and third baseman Billy Johnson to hit into a double play.

Bill Bevans hurls a one-hitter. (1947)

In the fourth inning, the Yankees scored again. Johnson led off with a single and left fielder Johnny Lindell followed with a double that knocked the runner in. But Gregg stiffened, allowing no more runs, and it was 2–0 after four-and-a-half innings.

The Dodgers got one run back in their half of the fifth. Bevans, who had not permitted a hit up to this point, walked both Dodger third baseman Spider Jorgenson and Gregg to open the stanza. Second baseman Eddie Stanky bunted them along. With a two-run lead, Yankee manager Bucky Harris decided to play the infield back. Thus when Reese grounded out to Rizzuto, Jorgenson scored, and the hitless Dodgers trailed by only 2–1.

As the innings wore on, Bevans did his best to disguise the fact that the Dodgers were still hitless. His pitching was not an artistic masterpiece. He walked ten men, four of them leading off an inning. In addition, there were numerous fine plays behind him. In the very first inning, second baseman Stirnweiss robbed Reese of a base hit with a stop and throw from behind second base that drew applause even from the partisan Dodger crowd. In the second inning, left fielder Johnny Lindell fell into the stands catching a ball hit by Jackie Robinson. Dodger left fielder Gene Hermanski was robbed of two extra base hits, once by DiMaggio and once by Henrich. Henrich's play, coming in the eighth inning, loomed large. The Yankees' herculean efforts were not only keeping them in the lead, but moving their pitcher along toward immortality—the first no-hitter in Series history.

The Yankees attempted to add to their lead in the top of the ninth. Lindell opened the inning with a single off Hank Behrman, the Dodgers' third pitcher of the day. The left fielder was forced at second by Rizzuto. The Yankee shortstop made it to second, however, when he outran Behrman's throw to the keystone sack on Bevans' poor sacrifice bunt attempt. With first and second, Stirnweiss singled to short center, Rizzuto holding at third. Here, once again, Shotton called on Hugh Casey. Again Casey held the New York team off. With the dangerous Henrich at the plate, Casey threw one pitch, a double play ball, and the inning was over. The stage was thus set. Going into the last half of the ninth inning, the Dodgers were trailing 2–1, and they were still hitless.

Floyd "Bill" Bevans was two weeks short of his thirty-first birthday as he took the mound in the last of the ninth. The big man from Oregon had joined the Yankees during the 1944 season and compiled a 40–36 lifetime record. This season had been his worst, his record only 7–13. Still, manager Bucky Harris had confidence in him. That's why he decided to start him in this game. Little did anyone realize that after today Bevans would make only one more appearance in a major-league uniform. A mysterious arm ailment in 1948 ended his big-league pitching career.

Catcher Bruce Edwards opened the ninth for the Dodgers by smashing one of Bevans' deliveries. The crowd roared as the ball flew toward the left field seats. But the roar became a moan when Johnny Lindell, his back pressed against the wall, caught the screaming liner for out number one. Before Bevans could take a deep breath, Carl Furillo walked and once again the Yankee pitcher was doing his balancing act. Reserve outfielder Al Gionfriddo went in to run for Furillo. When Spider Jorgensen fouled out for the second out, it looked as if Bevans might be home free.

The Dodgers' hopes now rested with Pete Reiser, batting for Hugh Casey. Reiser, Brooklyn's regular center fielder, had suffered a leg injury the day before, forcing him out of the starting lineup today. He came to the plate limping noticeably. With the count two balls and one strike, Gionfriddo boldly broke for second and stole the bag. Now the situation was different. There was a runner on second, in scoring position, and a three-ball, one-strike count on Reiser. Bucky Harris ordered Bevans to give Reiser a fourth ball intentionally. In doing that, Harris opened himself up to endless second guessing. As far as the baseball purists were concerned, he had done the unforgiveable. He had put the winning run on base in the ninth inning.

Reserve infielder Eddie Miksis went in to run for Reiser. With Eddie Stanky due up next, Shotton went to his bench and called on 34-year-old veteran Ebbets Field favorite, Cookie Lavagetto. Though there wasn't much difference in their averages, Shotton reasoned that Lavagetto had more power than Stanky and he wanted power up there now.

Harry "Cookie" Lavagetto began his pro career in his hometown of Oakland, California in 1933. The following year, he was in the majors with the Pittsburgh Pirates. In 1937, he moved over to Brooklyn where he spent the rest of his playing days.

Lavagetto appeared in more than 1,000 big-league games, but if you ask the folks in Brooklyn, they remember only one. October 3, 1947 is still a cherished memory.

Despite the mess that Bevans had pitched himself into, Bucky Harris decided to stay with him. Maybe it was because he had gotten out of all the previous trouble he had been in today. Maybe it was a hunch. Whatever the reason, Bevans went to work on Lavagetto.

His first pitch was way outside, but Lavagetto, somewhat affected by the tension of the moment, swung and missed the ball by a foot. He didn't miss the next pitch. Meeting Bevans' outside fastball perfectly, he drove it off the scoreboard in right field. By the time Yankee outfielder Tommy Henrich got the ball into the infield, both Gionfriddo and Miksis had scored, and the Dodgers had tied the series at two games each. It was also the last base hit that Lavagetto would ever get in the majors.

A normal team might have folded under the heartbreak of such a loss. But the Yankees weren't a normal team. Taking the field the next day, they beat the Dodgers 2–1 behind the strong pitching of 27-year-old rookie right hander Frank "Spec" Shea. Shea, winning for the second time in this series, not only pitched a complete game, a four-hitter, but he also had two hits and an r.b.i.

As usual, when greatness was needed, the Yankees had Joe DiMaggio to go to. The "Yankee Clipper" hit a ball into the Ebbets Field seats in the fifth inning, which proved to be the winning run.

Harry "Cookie" Lavagetto. (1947)

Game Six was the Dodgers turn to rebound. They grabbed a four-run lead early, saw the Yankees tie them in the fourth, and move ahead 5–4 in the fifth. But the Dodgers came back with four in the sixth to take a 8–5 lead into the last half of that inning. Now it was the Yankees turn to put on the heat. With two men out, they had two men on base, and Joe DiMaggio was the batter. Again in a key spot, DeMaggio crushed the ball. The horsehide headed to the deepest part of left center field, out by the Yankee bullpen. It was a sure homer, and the score would be tied. Only it wasn't a homer. At the start of the inning, Shotton had put Gionfriddo in for defensive purposes. The manager looked like a prophet when the fleet center fielder made a miraculous catch on the long drive just as it was clearing the 415-foot marker and leaving the field. The catch, one of the most memorable and thrilling in World Series history, saved the game for Brooklyn and forced a seventh contest.

When the Dodgers jumped off to a two-run lead in the second inning, it seemed possible that the long drought was over and Brooklyn would finally have a World Series winner. But the Dodgers never scored again that day, as the Yankees received a wonderful long relief stint from ace fireman Joe Page. When Tommy Henrich knocked in the winning run for the third time in the Series, the Yankees had their 11th World Championship.

WILLIE MAYS AND
DUSTY RHODES LEAD
THE UNDERDOG GIANTS TO A
SWEEP OVER CLEVELAND—1954

A breath of fresh air swept American League baseball in 1954. The strangle hold the Yankees held on the rest of the league was relaxed, at least for one season. After winning five consecutive American League pennants and five World Series, the Yankees had been beaten by the Cleveland Indians. This was not just any Indian team. It was very likely the best team in the history of the franchise. The Yankees won 103 games in 1954. None of manager Casey Stengel's five championship teams ever won that many games. To beat the New Yorkers, the boys from the banks of Lake Erie won 111 games, an American League record. They had a pitching staff that was the toast of baseball. Three Hall-of-Famers were members of the mound crew.

The Indians' attack had several special individuals also. Second baseman Bobby Avila was the American League batting champ that year with a .341 average. Center fielder Larry Doby was the league's home-run and r.b.i. leader. Al Rosen, down slightly from the previous season's near triple-crown year, was still a force. So was first baseman Vic Wertz, a wonderful early season pickup from Baltimore.

The National League also had a new champion in 1954. The New York Giants had dethroned the Dodgers in a typically wacky and torrid pennant race between the two ancient and bitter rivals. That meant even without the Yankees or Dodgers, the city of New York still had a representative in the World Series.

Going into the Series, the Indians were overwhelming favorites to strip the Giants' gears. Not only had they solidly defeated the once-invincible Yankees, they had won 14 more games this season than the Giants had. It seemed unlikely the National League champs would fare any better against Cleveland's pitching than the American League batters had.

Looking back, it is easy to see how underrated the Giants were. Their numbers were less than the Indians' because their struggle was harder. Once again, as has happened so often since the end of World War II, the National League had a very tough pennant race. Some years, the pennant pressure hardened a team for the World Series battle. Other teams were destroyed by the struggle to get to the Series, and had little left when playing their American League foe. The 1951 New York Giants are a good example of the latter. They won their pennant in the last half of the ninth inning of the last game of a play-off series. They had given their all catching the Brooklyn Dodgers. At one point, they were 13½ games behind them. Leo Durocher's players gave a good account of themselves for three games, then collapsed. On the other hand, Durocher's 1954 unit was hardened by the hand-to-hand combat with the Dodgers.

The other National League teams pulled hard for the Giants in this Series. The league was suffering from a bad case of embarrassment, having lost the last seven Series in a row. The league office would have probably preferred the Dodgers carrying the league colors. But the Giants it was.

The first game of the Series was played at New York's historic old Polo Grounds. Giant fans had confidence in their team. They had seen them storm from behind time after time this year, winning games the other side had already counted in their win column.

The first-game pitchers were Cleveland's Bob Lemon and New York's Sal "The Barber" Maglie. Maglie was a tough customer, a man who had earned his nickname by his willingness to "shave" batters—that is, throw close to them. Lemon had had an outstanding year, Maglie only very good. Lemon had won 23 games, Maglie only 14. A former infielder, Lemon threw an excellent sinking fastball that batters usually slammed into the ground.

The Indians started the first inning of the first game as if they meant to make the Giants their 112th victim. Leadoff batter Al Smith, the left fielder, was nicked by a Maglie pitch. Already the Barber was sending Cleveland a message: don't crowd the plate. Second batter Bobby Avila obviously didn't get the message as he stepped into the first pitch and banged it to left field for a single. With Larry Doby and Al Rosen coming up, things looked grim early for New York. But Maglie was able to get both men to pop up to the infield, and it looked as if he would get out of the inning with no damage. The Tribe's fifth batter was Vic Wertz, a good hitter with excellent power. He promptly smacked a hanging curve to deep left center for a triple. In any other major-league ballpark, his drive would have been a three-run homer. But the Polo Grounds had a center field that was 484 feet at its deepest, the longest stretch of land in baseball. Down the lines, the distances were barely more than Little League. A drive of 279 feet was a homer down the left-field line. A 257-foot poke to the right-field foul pole was also a homer.

The dimensions of the Polo Grounds thus saved the Giants a run when Wertz died on third. The Indians' first-game offense died on third with him. The Giants tied the score in the third. Singles by first baseman Whitey Lockman, shortstop Alvin Dark and third baseman Hank Thompson, plus a walk to center fielder Willie Mays produced two runs.

For the next four innings, the teams took turns trying to push across the lead run. Each got men on base, but no runs were scored. In the eighth, the Indians started a rally that seemed as if it would lead to victory. Larry Doby began the inning by coaxing Maglie for a walk. Al Rosen then singled to deep shortstop. With runners on first and second and nobody out, that was all for Maglie. The 37-year-old veteran, despite not having one of his better pitching days, had kept the Giants in the game on sheer will power and fast fielding. But now Vic Wertz was coming to the plate again, and he had hit Maglie freely all day. In addition to his first-inning triple, Wertz also had two singles to his credit. Left-hander Don Liddle was Durocher's choice to face the left-handed hitter in this situation.

What happened next was one of the most thrilling moments in World Series history. Wertz stepped into one of Liddle's offerings and really laced it. The ball went to the deepest part of the ballpark, dead center field. Observers were sure the ball carried at least 460 feet from home plate. Everyone in the press box had already totaled at least two more runs on the Cleveland side of the ledger. They should have been watching Willie Mays rather than their scorebooks. The fabulous "Say-Hey Kid", already ranked at 23 among the greatest defensive center fielders ever to play the game, turned his back to the plate and galloped. He ran more than 100 feet when he made an over-the-head basket catch just short of the center-field bleacher wall. Mays pulled up short to avoid crashing into the wall, spun around quickly, and unleashed a mighty throw. Though he wasn't able to prevent Doby from moving over to third after the catch, Mays did hold Rosen at first. The Indians were shocked. Instead of having a two-run lead and a man on third base with no outs, they had first and third, one out, and the score was still tied. When the Giants wriggled out of the inning with the Indians failing to score, the New Yorkers exuded the extra confidence that goes with being a winner.

The Indians, whether they sensed it or not, were dead. They put men on base in both the ninth and tenth innings, but came away empty both times. The Giants also had a rally going in the ninth, but their attempt to win the game in this frame also fizzled.

Willie Mays makes a spectacular catch. (1954)

Right fielder Don Mueller opened up the last half of the tenth inning by striking out. Then Lemon made a fatal error by walking Mays, who stole second base on the first pitch to Hank Thompson. With the winning run in scoring position and one out, Cleveland manager Al Lopez had Thompson walked intentionally. Due up next was Monte Irvin, once a great ballplayer, but now at age 35, a mere shadow of his former self. During the season, Durocher had often used left-handed hitter Jim "Dusty" Rhodes as a pinch hitter for Irvin. Rhodes' 1954 statistics included a .341 batting average and 15 homers in only 164 times at bat. As a pinch hitter, the Alabama-born ballplayer had hit .333, winning numerous games with late-inning hits. When the game was on the line, Rhodes had come through time and again. Starting one of the most impressive streaks of clutch hitting in World Series history, Rhodes picked out one of Bob Lemon's sinkers and lifted it off the ground. Not far off the ground—no one would ever have mistaken the hit for a rocket launched to the moon. Rather it resembled a bird injured in flight. But it traveled far enough to suit Dusty's purposes. As the ball continued to gain altitude, the joy the Indians felt about an easy out changed to horror. Though Rhodes' drive was neither high nor far, it was placed perfectly. It was heading for the Polo Grounds' right-field wall. If the ball traveled 265 feet, it traveled a lot. With total disbelief on their faces, the American League champions watched as the ball just made it into the first row, over the outstretched glove of Indian right fielder Dave Pope. The parachute job hit a fan in the first row and bounced back onto the field. Rhodes' winning homer traveled half the distance Wertz' eighth-inning drive did. Nevertheless, Rhodes' homer which won the game, was one of the most thrilling moments in World Series history.

Game Two started out in a manner similar to Game One. Before the sounds of the national anthem had faded away, Al Smith had hit Johnny Antonelli's first pitch for a homer. The Indians broke on top again. Antonelli, who had been the Giants' ace lefthander all season, pitched a strange game this day. The 21-game winner struck out nine, walked six, and gave up eight hits. He was in constant trouble and pitched like a man on a tightrope. In the clutch, however, somehow he always came up with the right pitch. The home run he gave to Smith was the only run he allowed all day. For the second straight day, the Indians stranded 13 runners on the base paths.

Cleveland started star right-hander Early Wynn, a pitcher so tough he once boasted he would knock down his own grandmother if she crowded the plate. If it had worked out that any game of this Series became a Wynn versus Maglie match up, that would have been a dangerous day for batters.

From the start, Wynn had his good stuff going for him. Over the first four innings Wynn retired the 12 batters he faced. Mays finally broke his perfect spell with a leadoff walk in the fifth. Then Thompson lined a single to right, ending any

Dusty Rhodes belts a tenth-inning homer. (1954)

thoughts of a no-hitter. Durocher, a manager who liked to play hunches, decided to play his trump card again. He sent Dusty Rhodes up to bat for Monte Irvin. Once again, Rhodes got a hit. Though only a single this time, his line smash to right center scored Mays with the tying run. A few minutes later, the Giants pushed over a second run and took a 2–1 lead after five.

The score remained 2–1 until Rhodes came up in the seventh. Durocher had inserted him in left field when Irvin came out, then prayed nothing would be hit his way. Rhodes was a notoriously poor fielder. As luck would have it, nothing did come his way, except for a pitch from Early Wynn. Rhodes jumped all over the fastball and drove it against the upper-deck facade in deep right field for his third straight run-scoring hit. The final score of the second game was Giants 3, Indians 1. The Giants led the Series 2–0.

Though the scene shifted to Cleveland the next day, the script remained the same. In front of 71,555 people, the Giants scored a run in the first inning off starter Mike Garcia. Known as "The Big Bear," Garcia was the third member of Cleveland's reknowned "Big Three." Unfortunately for him, he didn't fare any better than his friends. In the third inning, both he and his Indian teammates collapsed, for all intents and purposes ending the Series.

Dark started the Giant third with a single. Hank Majeski, filling in for the ailing Al Rosen at third base, creeped in, expecting Don Mueller to bunt. It was the logical thing to expect. But unlike Cleveland manager Al Lopez, Durocher wasn't playing it safe. He had Mueller, a great placement hitter who had batted .342 that year, swing away on a hit and run. The ball sizzled past the startled Majeski. When Mays tapped a ball down the third base line, Dark was trapped in a run-down and tagged out. He was in the run-down long enough, however, to allow Mueller to get to third and Mays to second. Lopez ordered Thompson walked again. Again Rhodes pinch-hit for Irvin. Again he singled, knocking in two more runs. It was his fourth straight hit of the Series, and he had knocked in seven runs. The Series was over. Rhodes had taken the final piece of heart out of the Indians. The Giants won that game 6-2, and easily won the fourth game 7-4. It was one of the most astonishing sweeps in World Series annals.

SANDY AMOROS' CATCH
SAVES THE DODGERS' FIRST
WORLD CHAMPIONSHIP—1955

The 1955 World Series was another "Subway Series." Once again, the participants were the Yankees and the Dodgers. It was the sixth time in 15 years that the interborough rivals battled for the championship of the baseball world. Each of the five previous encounters had been won by the "Bronx Bombers." The borough of Brooklyn ached for revenge. But since both teams had essentially the same personnel as when they last met in 1953, the experts predicted the usual result.

That's not to say people didn't recognize the Dodgers as a very good team. Many thought the reason they lost every fall was a kind of hex. How else could you explain a team that had such great players as Roy Campanella, Duke Snider, Jackie Robinson, Pee Wee Reese, and Gil Hodges, always losing to anybody?

The Dodgers lost the first two games of the 1955 Series. Since no team up to then had ever lost the first two games and come back to win, Dodger fans were already lighting funeral candles and exclaiming, "Wait till next year!"

The third game was played in Brooklyn, and the Dodgers began to get well at home. Behind the slants of Johnny Podres, a 23-year-old left-hander from upstate New York, the Dodgers beat the Yanks, 8-3. Roy Campanella was the Dodger hitting star that day. The rotund catcher knocked in three runs with three hits, including a single, a double, and a home run.

The following day, the Dodger run-making machine again totaled eight, as they beat New York 8-5. The Dodger hitting attack was devastating. Campanella, Hodges, and Snider hit homers, forcing Yankee skipper Casey Stengel to use five pitchers. Suddenly, the Series was tied at two games each, and Yankee fans were gloomy, while Dodger rooters whooped it up.

That 1955 season had been wonderful for the Dodgers. The team had gotten off to the best start in National League history. They won their first 10 games of the season, lost two out of three to the Giants, then won 11 more in a row. After 24 games, they were 22-2. No team mounted a serious threat to their lead all season. They won the pennant by 13½ games. They scored nearly 100 runs more than any other senior-circuit team. They hit more than 200 homers, while also leading the league in team stolen bases. Four players—Snider with 42, Campanella with 32, Hodges with 27, and Furillo with 26—hit more than 20 homers. All but Furillo knocked in more than 100 runs.

The fifth game of the 1955 World Series was critical for the Dodgers. If they were going to have a real chance at finally winning a World Series, they had to go back to Yankee Stadium one game up. Roger Craig and Clem Labine combined to hold New York to three runs and six hits, and the Dodgers won 5–3. Again Brooklyn power turned the trick. A homer by left fielder Sandy Amoros and two by Duke Snider accounted for four of the five runs.

The Dodgers had come home trailing two games to none. Now they were going back to the big Bronx ball yard up 3–2. Their fans in Brooklyn dared to hope for the best, though half-expecting the worst.

They had good reason to expect the worst. The Yankees had won the last seven Series they had played in. They had won 13 out of the last 14 Series they had played in. They had never lost a World Series to Brooklyn. They knew how to win when the pressure was the greatest.

In Game Six, the Yankees came out smoking. They scored all five of their runs in the first inning. They banged Dodger rookie left-hander Karl Spooner, manager Walter Alston's surprise starter, out of the box before the first inning was over. Alston, a first-year manager, bypassed his regular-season ace, Don Newcombe, who won 20 games that year, for Spooner. Newcombe had been his first-game starter, but had been shelled by the Yankees. He had given up six runs in less than six innings. He had a history of World Series failure. Alston, hoping to be able to steal a game, and the Series, gambled with the rookie and lost.

All over Brooklyn that night, people couldn't sleep. They knew that tomorrow their "Beloved Bums" would be executed by the hated Yankee machine again. As hard as they tried to be optimistic, they had to face facts. When the money was on the line, the Dodgers never beat the Yankees.

At 3:44 P.M., on the afternoon of October 4, 1955, over 50 years of frustration ended. That's when Gil Hodges caught Pee Wee Reese's throw, and the Dodgers had finally won a World Series. They had beaten the Yankees at Yankee Stadium in the seventh and deciding game, 2–0. They had finally won a World Series on their eighth try. They won even though an injury forced Jackie Robinson to miss the final game. They won even though an injury caused Duke Snider to play the final game with a limp. There were other heroes to fill in for the wounded Flatbush stars.

Brooklyn's number-one hero that afternoon was the kid left-hander from Witherbee, New York, Johnny Podres. It was Podres who pitched the shutout victory.

Hero number two was Gil Hodges, the power-hitting, smooth-fielding first baseman, who knocked in both Brooklyn runs with a single and a sacrifice fly.

Hero number three was Sandy Amoros, who was a national hero in Cuba by the time dusk fell. With two on and no one out in the last of the sixth inning, Amoros made a game-saving, lunging, one-handed catch on a fly ball hit into the left-field corner by Yogi Berra. He then quickly got the ball into the infield, and the Yankee runner at first was doubled up.

Even though Podres hurled a shutout, he didn't have an easy game. New York had runners on constantly. Alston was at the mound almost as much as Podres. Not all the trouble was his fault. In the fourth inning, both Duke Snider and left fielder Jim Gilliam (who moved to second base in the sixth, Amoros taking his defensive position) hesitated, expecting the other one to grab Yogi Berra's pop fly into short left center. The ball dropped between them for a double, putting Berra on second with no outs. Dodger fans, as usual, expected the worst. But Podres buckled down and knocked off the next three hitters without letting Berra advance at all.

Tommy Byrne was the Yankee pitcher. The left-hander, who once had difficulty finding the plate, but became a good pitcher once he mastered control, had won the Series' second game. In this game, he matched goose eggs with Podres through the fourth. In that frame, Campanella hit a sizzling shot down the third-base line and into the left-field corner for a double. It was Brooklyn's first hit of the game. Campy reached third as Furillo did his job and grounded out to the right side. A few minutes later, Campanella tallied as Hodges whacked a single to left.

In the sixth inning, Pee Wee Reese, a Dodger for all five of Brooklyn's World Series defeats at New York's hands, led off with a single. He reached second on Snider's sacrifice bunt. Snider himself was safe when he brushed the ball out of Yankee first baseman Bill Skowron's hands. Campanella then sacrificed the runners along. Casey Stengel, playing the obvious percentages, walked Furillo to load the bases and set up a double-play opportunity. Hodges ruined his strategy by lifting a long fly ball to left center, which scored Reese from third.

One thing you knew when you were playing a Yankee team in the 1950s was how dangerous they were late in a game. The New Yorkers had become famous for five o'clock lightning. Often they would be behind in a game, and in either the eighth or ninth inning, they would erupt with a flurry of home runs to win.

Though it was only 3:00, the Yankees began to put a rally together in their sixth turn at bat. Second baseman Billy Martin led off with a walk. Third baseman Gil McDougald completely fooled the Dodger infield by beating out a bunt single. A roar went through the Yankee Stadium crowd of 62,465 as they anticipated what would happen. Here it was again, a Yankee rally and the inevitable Dodger downfall. When Berra sliced a fly ball into the left-field corner, heads nodded and tongues wagged. One run would score for sure, and very likely two. If the Yankees tied the score here, could the winning run be far behind?

There was one factor missing from this view. The Dodgers had made some line-up changes after their turn at bat in the top half of the inning. Among the moves, Gilliam moved to second base and was replaced by Sandy Amoros in left field. The fleet Amoros got on his horse when Berra slapped the ball. He galloped madly from left center, where he had been playing the pull-hitting catcher. Just as the ball was about to land, he stuck out his glove and caught the ball. The crowd was thunderstruck. So was Gil McDougald, the runner who had been on first. The Yankee third baseman, a thorough professional allowed himself to be doubled off first and the inning was over an instant later when Bauer grounded out.

It was a lucky break for the Dodgers that Amoros was in left field. Sandy was a left-handed thrower. Gilliam, whom he replaced in the outfield, was a right-hander. Amoros' catch couldn't have been made by a right-hander. The fact that Amoros had his glove on his right hand allowed him to reach the ball.

Real champs go down hard, and that's exactly what the Yankees did. In the seventh inning, left fielder Elston Howard singled and Mickey Mantle, who was crippled with a bad leg throughout the Series, came up as a pinch hitter. The sight of his broad back with the number seven on it set Yankee fans to dancing joyfully. They had visions of the Oklahoma Kid parking one of his tape-measure home runs in a deep recess of Yankee Stadium. It was not to be. Batting for pitcher Bob Grim, Mantle popped up. The Yankees still managed to load the bases that inning, but Podres called on all his skill and cunning and turned away Berra and Bauer with the tying and lead runs on base.

In the last of the ninth inning, Podres got Skowron, Bob Cerv, and Howard one, two, three. The Dodgers were finally World Champions. Never had a group of fans cared so much about their team winning the championship as the Brooklyn Dodger fans did. It was no surprise that, when the game ended with the Dodgers victorious, the borough of Brooklyn went totally crazy. Confetti poured out of office windows in the downtown business district. Cars tooted their horns non-stop, and large crowds gathered on street corners. It was Christmas, New Year's Eve, and the Fourth of July in October. It was the happiest day in the borough of Brooklyn since the end of the war.

Sandy Amoros nabs the ball at the fence. (1955)

"I knew we would win it today," said young Podres later to the hundreds of news reporters who were gathered around him. "I told that to everybody. I told Pee Wee. Ask Pee Wee."

Reporters immediately trooped over to the veteran Dodger shortstop. "That's true," Reese agreed. "John was real confident, much more so than me. I had seen the worm turn too often. When I was standing at shortstop in the last half of the ninth, I kept saying to myself, 'This can't be true. This can't be true. Something has to happen to make us lose.' Something had always happened before. But nothing happened and when Gilly [Hodges] caught my throw to end the game I had all I could do to keep from crying. I've been trying to beat these guys since 1941. That's a long time."

It had been a long time indeed.

DON LARSEN'S
PERFECT GAME—1956

One year later, the autumn playmates were back at it again. The Dodgers faced the Yankees for the seventh time in 16 years. The World Championship of baseball seemed to be nothing more than a private, intercity tournament. Clearly, New York and Brooklyn were the class teams of their leagues at that time. The Dodgers had been developed by the genius of Branch Rickey. After signing Jackie Robinson, he obtained the signatures of several other talented black athletes. Roy Campanella, Don Newcombe, and Junior Gilliam were part of the backbone of several pennant-winning teams. In 1952, right-handed pitcher Joe Black was the best pitcher in the National League as he almost singlehandedly led the Dodgers to the championship.

Rickey's assembly-like farm system pushed out white stars by the dozen. Men like Snider, Hodges, Furillo, plus pitchers like Carl Erskine and Clem Labine moved step by step up the Dodger organizational ladder. This combination of farm-system products and blacks from the Negro Leagues gave Brooklyn the post-World War II dynasty team that became immortalized as "the Boys of Summer."

For 40 years, the Yankees were the richest team in baseball. They bought the best players available. When farm systems came into vogue, they built one of the biggest and most productive. Until the 1950s, however, they signed only the most talented white players. They nurtured their young, brought them along slowly, and just when one star would wear out, another would fit in.

Late in the season, however, the Yankees had a different philosophy. If the team was in the midst of a close pennant race, they would invariably take the rubber band off their huge bankroll and buy an older player or two from a team out of contention. Former stars like first baseman Johnny Mize, outfielder Enos Slaughter, and pitcher Johnny Sain, to name just three, were at the tag end of their careers when they were purchased by the Yankees. But they still could perform enough of their former magic in key situations to help the New Yorkers win several pennants.

In 1954, the Yankees and the Baltimore Orioles, a struggling franchise that had moved from St. Louis just the year before, pulled off a huge 18-player trade. The two most important people coming to the Yankees were right-handed pitchers "Bullet" Bob Turley, the American League strikeout leader in 1954, and Don Larsen. Larsen, 6' 4" and 220 pounds, had won only three games and lost 21 in 1954, but Yankee scouts liked his arm and his size. They felt that, with proper teaching and a good team behind him, he could be a big winner.

The Yankee scouts who recommended Larsen looked exceptionally smart after the 1955 season. The big Californian won 18 games, lost only three that year. He was 9-2 with the Yankees, and 9-1 with their top farm club at Denver. He seemed to be on his way. But Don Larsen was not the type of man who could stand prosperity. There was a streak of wildness in him that usually ended with Larsen hurting himself.

Larsen had had a checkered career since coming into organized baseball in 1947. After he strung together those good numbers in 1955, the Yankee publicity department put out stories on the "New Larsen"—a serious, dedicated Larsen. The only trouble was the "New Larsen" wasn't much different from the old one. One morning during spring training in 1956, he not only broke curfew, he ran his car into a tree at 5:30 A.M. He was unhurt, but the glowing reports about the "New Larsen" weren't. They were immediately ditched.

It seemed as if 1956 would be just another year in Larsen's life. Certainly it hadn't started out much differently. Once again, people would call him a playboy. Once again, they would look at his fastball and his size and wonder why he wasn't a dominating pitcher. In fact, he was terribly inconsistent. He would give an excellent performance, then a poor one, then an indifferent one, then a good one. Casey Stengel never knew what to expect when he handed him the ball. Usually, he had control problems. It was the inability to have good control of his pitches on a regular basis that led Larsen to change his pitching motion drastically. Late in the 1956 season, Larsen began pitching without a wind-up. The new way seemed to improve Larsen's control and his effectiveness. His September surge allowed him to improve his record to 11-5, and convinced Stengel to start him in the second game of the World Series.

The Yankees had taken the easy route to the Series, beating out their closest pursuer, Cleveland, by nine games. The Dodgers, on the other hand, took the hard road, winning a three-way flag fight on the final day. Don Newcombe had to beat Pittsburgh on the final Sunday of the season to clinch the pennant. This Dodger team hadn't played as well as the 1955 group. Experienced players like Reese, Robinson, and Campanella proved invaluable.

Brooklyn got the jump in the 1956 Series when Sal Maglie, the former Giant great whom Brooklyn had bought from Cleveland in midseason, won the first game 6-3. Maglie had pitched superbly for the Dodgers, compiling a 13-5 record. He was nearly invincible in September, pitching the first no-hitter of his career on September 25. All those years that Dodger fans hated the bearded man from Buffalo were quickly forgotten.

Leading the Dodgers' offense in the opening-game triumph was Gil Hodges. The big first baseman belted a three-run homer off Whitey Ford in the third inning. The score was tied 2-2 at the time. The Yankees never threatened after that, as Maglie held them at bay. Jackie Robinson also had a Dodger homer, while Mickey Mantle and Billy Martin accounted for all the Yankee runs with homers.

Game Two was another one of those October Dodger-Yankee donnybrooks. Because both teams possessed great hitting power, if the pitching was the slightest bit off, calculators were needed to total the score. Both starting pitchers, Don Larsen and Don Newcombe, were knocked out in the second inning. Newcombe left in the top of the second, with the Dodgers trailing 6-0. Larsen took leave of Ebbets Field in the last of the second, with two out and the score 6-4. After Larsen left, the Dodgers continued to swing destructive bats. They scored two more in the second to tie the score, then added seven more over the next few innings to win going away 13-8.

The scenario was exactly the reverse of last year. In 1955, the Dodgers had come into the Series easy pennant winners, and the Yanks had just scraped by. But the Yanks won the first two games on their home turf. This year, the Dodgers had just beaten out Milwaukee and Cincinnati, and then copped the first two games on Ebbets Field sod. Last year after two games, the talk was of a Yankee sweep. Now the talk was of a Dodger sweep.

The sweep talk stopped after Game Three. Back at Yankee Stadium, the perennial world champs got well. Behind Whitey Ford's solid pitching, and homers by Billy Martin and veteran National League outfielder Enos "Country" Slaughter, the Yanks won 5-3.

New York evened the Series at two games each in Game Four. Tommy Sturdivant's six-hit hurling and the hitting of Billy Martin, Mickey Mantle, and right fielder Hank Bauer led the Yanks to a very professional win. Martin knocked in the winning run, but it was Mantle who devastated the Dodgers with his long home run. It came as no surprise that the kid from Commerce, Oklahoma would be hitting homers in this Series. After all, he had hit homers and triples and doubles against everybody in the American League this year. Mantle, who first joined the Yankees in 1951 with the tag of future superstar written all over him, had finally lived up to his advance billing this year. He won the hitter's Triple Crown, banging out 52 homers, knocking in 130 runs, and hitting .353—all league highs. He was the most destructive offensive force the junior circuit had seen since Ted Williams was in his heyday.

The scheduled pitchers for Game Five were the Dodgers' first-game winner, Sal Maglie, and the Yankees Don Larsen. On the surface, the pitching match up seemed to be in the Dodgers' favor.

In the second game of the Series, Larsen had been wild. In less than two innings, he walked four men and gave up only one hit. Casey Stengel, looking for answers to explain Larsen's poor performance, thought the mound might have thrown him off. After all, it was a strange mound to him. The Yankees play in Ebbets Field only once a year, in October.

After Larsen changed his pitching motion and went to the no-windup delivery, he pitched four low-hit games back to back. Stengel decided he couldn't have gone sour all at once.

On this day, October 8, 1956, Larsen had pinpoint control. He went to a three-ball count only once, and that was in the first inning. He threw mostly fastballs and sliders, relying on power pitching. He made only 97 pitches, consistently getting the first pitch in for a strike. The defensive play behind him was excellent. In the second inning, Jackie Robinson bounced a hot shot off third baseman Andy Carey's glove. Gil McDougald, playing shortstop backed Carey up, retrieved the ball, and threw the Brooklyn player out.

In the fourth inning, fortune smiled on Larsen as a ball that Duke Snider hammered solidly went into the right-field seats, just foul. In the fifth, Gil Hodges drove a ball to deep left center, but Mantle made a nice backhanded catch, while running at full speed. The next batter, Sandy Amoros, then pulled a wicked line drive down the right-field line and into the seats. Like Snider's shot, this was foul by the scantest of margins.

Meanwhile, the Yankees weren't exactly tearing up Maglie either. The Dodger pitcher retired the first 11 batters he faced. With two out in the fourth, however, Mantle took him downtown with a homer into the right-field seats. His third homer of the Series gave the Yankees a 1–0 lead.

In the Yankee sixth, Andy Carey led off with a single, was sacrificed to second by Larsen and scored on Hank Bauer's single.

Entering the seventh inning, Larsen had retired all 18 batters he had faced. In Yankee Stadium, the 64,519 spectators could feel the tension rising. The historical possibilities didn't have to be spelled out.

Don Larsen shows his winning form. (1956)

As each Dodger made out, the crowd would applaud a little more intensely.

Larsen fought hard for baseball immortality. The Dodgers sent the top of their batting order up in the seventh. Junior Gilliam grounded out, Pee Wee Reese and Duke Snider hit lazy, fly-ball outs. Robinson opened the eighth, and Larsen put him out himself. Hodges hit a hard liner that Carey speared for the second out. Amoros flied to left. The Dodger eighth was over. Larsen was three outs away from a perfect game, a feat that had never been accomplished in Series action. In fact, a perfect game hadn't been pitched in the major leagues since 1922, 34 years before.

Veteran National League umpire Babe Pinelli was getting ready for the last inning he would ever work behind the plate in the major leagues. After 22 years as an arbiter, he had announced his retirement plans. His going-away present was a game that would never be forgotten.

Larsen took the mound in the ninth, showing no signs of the emotional turmoil that must have been raging inside of him. He faced the dangerous Carl Furillo to open the inning, and "Skoonj," who had hit .289 that year, with 21 homers and 83 r.b.i.'s, fouled off four consecutive pitches. Finally, after what seemed like a duel to the death, he lifted a fly ball to Hank Bauer in right. There was one out.

Roy Campanella was next. The rotund catcher ripped at Larsen's first fastball and banged it off the mezzanine facade. It was foul by plenty, but very well hit. On the next pitch, he tapped the ball weakly toward Billy Martin. The second baseman charged the ball, then carefully flipped it to first baseman Joe Collins.

The Dodgers had only one out left. With the pitcher's spot due, Brooklyn sent Dale Mitchell, a 10-year American League veteran, whose contract they had purchased in mid-season, to hit for Maglie. Mitchell, a lifetime .312 hitter, had batted against Larsen many times as a member of the Cleveland Indians. The Yankee hurler was no mystery to him. Worse, from Larsen's point of view, was that Mitchell was a slap hitter. A guy who could drive the ball to all fields was the hardest kind of hitter a pitcher had to face in this kind of situation.

Mitchell had played in two World Series as a member of the Cleveland Indians. He wouldn't choke in this situation. The pitch was outside—ball one. The crowd moaned. Mitchell waved his bat back and forth. Larsen looked for Berra's sign. He nodded, then fired the ball. Strike one was called as Mitchell swung and missed.

The crowd roared. It was deafening, but Larsen didn't hear any of it. He looked at Berra. When he saw the signal, he threw the next pitch. Pinelli's arm shot high into the air—strike two. The crowd roared again. Mitchell stepped out of the batter's box. Pinelli came around in front of the plate, pulled a whisk broom from out of his back pocket, and brushed home plate spotless. Larsen took off his cap and wiped the sweat from his brow. He turned away from the plate and faced the outfield. He fidgeted around, fingering the ball, then releasing his grip. He turned back to the plate and looked at Berra's signal again.

The crowd was in an uproar now. Larsen wound up and everybody held their breath. Mitchell swung and fouled it off. Larsen got the ball back from Berra. He wasted no time. He looked for the signal, nodded slightly and fired a pitch that was taken. From the press box, the pitch seemed high and a little outside. In the batter's box, Dale Mitchell felt the same way. But Babe Pinelli felt different. He shot his right arm into the air with authority. "Strike three!" he shouted. Larsen had pitched a perfect game. If people in the rest of the Bronx thought an earthquake was in progress, it was understandable. The people in Yankee Stadium went wild.

The victory gave the Yankees a 3-2 lead in the Series. It gave Larsen lasting fame. But Larsen's no-hitter was immediately yesterday. The following day, the Dodgers shook off whatever aftereffects his master-piece might have had on them, and they beat New York 1-0 in ten innings. It was a remarkable performance by a gutty team.

The Yankees also had one last remarkable performance left in 1956. They won Game Seven 9-0, with Yogi Berra hitting two homers. The Yankees were the champions of the baseball world again, after a hiatus of three years. Few remember that. But Don Larsen's perfect game, one of the most thrilling moments in World Series history, will never be forgotten.

BOB GIBSON STRIKES OUT
SEVENTEEN MEN—1968

In the long history of baseball, no pitcher ever had a better year than Bob Gibson of the St. Louis Cardinals had in 1968. The big, 33-year-old right-hander from Omaha, Nebraska won 22 games and lost 9. He pitched 13 shutouts, five of them in succession. At one point, he had 48 consecutive scoreless innings, a streak ended by a wild pitch. He gave up only two earned runs in a 95-inning stretch. His 1.12 earned-run average broke the National League record of 1.22 set in 1915 by Grover Cleveland Alexander. After getting off to a slow start and compiling an early-season 3–5 record, he won 15 games in a row. He pitched 28 complete games and was never knocked out of the box in his 34 starts. His 268 strikeouts led the league. He won both the Cy Young Award and the Most Valuable Player Award.

In the American League, Detroit's 24-year-old Dennis McLain was also having a dream season. McLain won 31 games, the first major-league pitcher to win 30 or more since Dizzy Dean won 30 for the St. Louis Cardinals in 1934. He struck out 280 to lead the majors in that category. Like Gibson, McLain won both the prestigious Cy Young Award as the best pitcher in the American League, and the American League's Most Valuable Player Award. The match up between the two in the World Series was inevitable and seemed made in heaven.

The 1968 World Series was Denny McLain's first, but Bob Gibson had already been the star pitcher in the 1964 and 1967 fall classics. In 1964, he pitched three complete games, winning two of them, including the seventh-game clincher. In 27 innings that year, he struck out 31 Yankee batters.

Again in 1967, he pitched three complete games, this time winning all three, striking out 26 men in 27 innings. Once again, he won the deciding game over the Boston Red Sox. Coming into the 1968 interleague showdown, Gibson had won five consecutive World Series games, all complete games. He had already established himself as one of the all-time World Series pitching greats.

Both St. Louis and Detroit made it to the World Series easily. Neither team had to play a crucial series in September. Detroit won the American League pennant by 12 games. St. Louis clinched their pennant by nine. Because the Cardinals were the defending World Champions, most people expected them to win again.

On October 2, 1968, a confrontation between the two great pitchers took place. On that warm, sunny, fall day, Detroit's first batter was a left-hander, Dick McAuliffe. The second baseman had led the American League in runs scored with 95. He banged out 50 extra base hits, 16 of them homers. He was a factor with a bat in his hands.

The first time up facing Gibson, McAuliffe was no factor. The Cardinal pitcher blew him out of the box on a swinging third strike. He did the same thing one out later to Hall-of-Famer Al Kaline. Bob Gibson was off and running.

If Gibson was running in the first inning, he was positively sprinting in the second. He faced three good hitters—Norm Cash, Willie Horton, and Jim Northrup,—and each went down on strikes. In the third, all-star catcher Bill Freehan and pitcher McLain bit the dust on strikes. Once through the Detroit batting order, and Gibson had seven strikeouts.

In the last half of the third, the Cardinals threatened to score as Lou Brock stole his first base of the Series and went to third on Freehan's wild throw. But McLain dug his heels in and escaped without a run scoring.

In the Tiger fourth, Gibson struck out Kaline again, his eighth. In the last half of the inning, the Cards broke the scoreless tie, thanks in part to McLain losing the plate's geography. Roger Maris, who had hit 61 homers to break Babe Ruth's record in 1961, led off with a walk. After Orlando Cepeda, a great hitter during the regular season, but a man with a history of poor post-season performances, popped out, catcher Tim McCarver walked. Third baseman Mike Shannon lined a single to left field, scoring Maris, and when Horton fumbled the ball, McCarver went to third and Shannon to second. When the Tigers moved their infield in, Julian Javier's routine grounder sneaked past McAuliffe's lunge and became a single. The Cardinals led 3-0.

In the Tiger fifth, Gibson gave no signs of letting up. He struck out third baseman Don Wert, gave up no hits, and after five innings, had shut out Detroit on two hits, striking out nine.

The Tigers stirred a bit in the sixth inning. After a pinch hitter for McLain grounded out, McAuliffe grounded a single into right field. Mickey Stanley was Gibson's tenth strikeout victim, and the rally seemed blunted. But Al Kaline got hold of a rising fastball and hammered it into the left-field corner. Only fast fielding by Lou Brock held McAuliffe at third. With two runners in scoring position, Gibson went to work on the dangerous Norm Cash. Cash had once led the American League in batting average, banging out a .361 mark in 1961. He never again approached those numbers, but had the reputation of being a solid hitter who could hit a pitcher's mistake out of sight. Cash had hit .263 this year, with 25 homers in only 411 at bats. He was a dangerous man swinging the bat.

Taking hardly any time between pitches, Gibson fired fastball after fastball to the fastball-loving first baseman. In the power battle that ensued, the pitcher won. Norm Cash was the Tiger's 11th strikeout victim.

Denny McLain was gone as the last of the sixth opened. Pat Dobson, another right-hander, was Detroit manager Mayo Smith's choice as his replacement. Bob Gibson had won the long-awaited shootout.

In the top of the seventh, Gibson kept the Tigers at bay with monotonous regularity. Again he allowed no hits. Again he struck out two batters, this time Northrup and Freehan. His total rose to 13. Sandy Koufax' mark was in jeopardy.

In the last of the seventh, Lou Brock added another run to Gibson's working margin when he hit a homer into the right center-field bleachers. Curt Flood, the marvelous center fielder, followed his four bagger with a single and stole second. But Dobson pulled himself together and got Maris to pop to McAuliffe for the third out.

In the top of the eighth, the Tigers sent up Hall-of-Famer Eddie Mathews as a pinch swinger for Don Wert. Gibson and Mathews had faced each other numerous times when Mathews was a siege gun for both the Milwaukee and Atlanta Braves. Mathews had twice been a National League home-run champion and had hit 512 lifetime homers. Gibson pitched carefully to him. Finally, on a 2–2 pitch, he pumped a hard slider past the great veteran for the strikeout. That made 14 strikeouts. He got the next two men easily, but neither struck out, so entering the ninth, Gibson was one short of Koufax.

It was the top of the ninth, and Gibson wanted that strikeout record badly. He was on the verge of several records, but a strikeout mark held by Koufax, his chief rival for best pitcher of the era, would be sweet.

Detroit shortstop Mickey Stanley led off the ninth inning with a single and Gibson's thoughts quickly shifted from records to winning the game. Now the strength of the Tiger line-up was coming to the plate. It was a powerful line-up. Detroit had banged out 185 homers in 1968 and scored 671 runs. But Gibson, grim and businesslike, struck out Al Kaline to tie the record, Norm Cash to break it, and Willie Horton to add icing on the cake. He had gotten the strikeout record with a closing flourish.

Fireballing Bob Gibson sets a strikeout record. (1968)

After the game in the packed clubhouse, members of both teams talked about Gibson's thrilling performance. Though he gave up five hits, most agreed that this had to be the most overpowering World Series pitching performance since Don Larsen's perfect game 12 years before.

"I would have to say it was one of the best games Gibson ever threw," said St. Louis manager Red Schoendienst. "After all, how many pitchers strike out 17 batters? He's pitched just as well at other times, but he didn't get 17 strikeouts."

"It wasn't one of my best games," Bob Gibson disagreed. "It was, however, one of my most important. I could see they were surprised by my breaking ball. They were swinging at my curve like it was a fast ball. When I was behind on the count, I threw a lot of sliders. But most of my strikeouts were chalked up on the fastball."

"He was a great pitcher today," Al Kaline said. Kaline had gone one for four—three strikeouts and a double. "I guess he'll be one of the top pitchers who ever lived."

Suffering through the strange feeling of being ignored for one of the few times in 1968, Denny McLain added, "That was the greatest pitching performance I've ever seen by anybody."

Whatever the opinions, certain things Gibson did this day were written on stone tablets as new records. The victory was his sixth straight over three Series, tying a World Series record. It was also the sixth straight complete game he pitched. It was one of the most thrilling moments in World Series history.

For historical purposes, Gibson's opening-day show turned the rest of the Series into a ho-hum cluster of games. Left-hander Mickey Lolich, the Tiger's second-game starter, was their second best pitcher that year. The six-year major-league veteran had compiled a 17–9 record during the season, but he was overlooked because of McLain's enormous feat.

The World Series-hardened Cardinals were ready to move in for the kill in Game Two. Schoendienst nominated Nelson Briles as his second-game starter.

Detroit bounced back in Game Two with avenging fervor. They struck for 13 hits, including homers by Willie Horton, Norm Cash and, of all people, Mickey Lolich, his first big-league homer ever. The Tigers won easily, 8–1. Nelson Briles was used up by the fifth, and the Cardinals filled the last four innings with three mop-up pitchers.

The Cardinals' only bright spot this day was left fielder Lou Brock. The brilliant speedster stole two bases, one of them leading to St. Louis' only run. Game Two changed the face of the Series. Two things became firmly established in Cardinal minds. The first was that Tiger home-run power was no myth. Not even huge Busch Memorial Stadium could contain their long drives when they were stroking the ball well. The second newly accepted fact was that Mickey Lolich was better than his 17–9 season record indicated.

Game Three saw Cardinal power erupt in the smaller Detroit ballpark. Unlike Busch Memorial Stadium, which had only been open for two years,

Tiger Stadium was one of the old ballparks. It had gone through three name changes in its history, from Navin Field, to Briggs Stadium, to the present Tiger Stadium. Its right-field stands were fairly accessible to left-handed power. Though a right-handed hitter had to hit the ball further to get a homer, left field was also in range. Left-handed Tim McCarver and righty Orlando Cepeda both reached the seats with three-run homers that led the Cardinals to a 7–3 win.

Along with the power display, Lou Brock was instrumental in the St. Louis win. In the fifth inning, Brock singled to center and immediately stole second. He was knocked home by a Curt flood double. Several batters later, Tim McCarver belted his three-run shot, finishing off a rally started by Brock.

In Game Four, the Cardinals took a 3–1 lead in games, beating Detroit 10–1. Once again, Gibson was magnificent, pitching a five hitter, striking out 10. This was his seventh consecutive World Series, complete-game victory, a record.

It seemed certain the World Championship was returning to St. Louis. Again Brock was the offensive catalyst, smacking McLain's first pitch for a homer, stealing three more bases, and seemingly being everywhere Detroit didn't want him. McLain, if anything, was less of a puzzle to the St. Louis hitters this time. He allowed six hits and four runs in less than three innings. After Game Four, the score between the superpitchers stood Gibson 2, McLain 0.

In Game Five, the Cardinals started off as if this would be the day the Series was over. Brock led off against Lolich with a ringing double. Curt Flood singled and Cepeda hit a homer, and before most people were settled in their seats, the Cardinals led 3-0. But that was all the Cardinals would score off Lolich this day. With the Cardinals held in check, the Tigers began to peck away at Nelson Briles. They picked up two runs in the fourth inning and three more in the seventh and won 5-3. The Series headed back to St. Louis.

In Game Six, the Tigers split the Cardinals' gut, beating them 13-1. McLain, not having to face Gibson head up, finally won a game. In the third inning, the Tigers scored ten runs, smashing St. Louis starter Ray Washburn and three relief pitchers.

So it came to pass that there was a Game Seven, a Game Seven that just a few days before the Cardinals, and most everybody else in the baseball world, were sure would not be needed. The pitching match up was Gibson against Lolich, both 2-0 in this series. Zeroes filled the scorebook until the seventh inning. In that frame, the Tigers scored three runs when Curt Flood, then the best defensive center fielder in the game, misjudged a line drive with two on and two out. The mistake led to three runs. Each team added a run in the ninth, and suddenly the Tigers were the comeback World Champions of 1968. Lolich had won three games and hit a homer. He was superb in the clutch. But despite his heroics, the 1968 Series is best remembered for Bob Gibson's opening-game, 17-strikeout performance.

CARLTON FISK'S
TWELFTH-INNING HOMER
WINS SIXTH SERIES GAME—1975

Everyone who saw the 1975 World Series was overwhelmed by it. Old-timers, who generally have nothing good to say about modern baseball, admitted they were impressed by the quality of play. New-comers to the sport were able to see baseball at its best. Experts who had written about the game for more than a few years ran out of superlatives to describe this fall classic. For that's what it was—a true fall classic. Even the ballplayers who were in it were impressed by what they were doing. In the tenth inning of the sixth game, Cincinnati's Pete Rose bent over and whispered to Boston's catcher, Carlton Fisk, "Wow, this is some kind of game. Some kind of Series. I'm sure glad I'm playing in it. It really is fun." No one who saw it will ever forget the 1975 Series.

The Cincinnati Reds played the Boston Red Sox in the 72nd edition of the World Series. The Reds were a powerful veteran club that had already won two National League pennants, plus one divisional title in the 1970s. They had easily captured the National League West divisional title, finishing 20 games ahead of Los Angeles. They won 108 games, lost only

54 for a .667 percentage. They clinched their divisional championship on September 7, the earliest any National League team had ever mathematically clinched a title.

The Reds then defeated the Pittsburgh Pirates, winners of the National League East, in three straight play-off games. Even before the 1975 Series began, people were calling the Reds one of the great ball clubs of all time. Their roster was dotted with Hall-of-Fame candidates, like second baseman Joe Morgan, the league's Most Valuable Player that year, third baseman Pete Rose, catcher Johnny Bench, left fielder George Foster, and first baseman Tony Perez. All-stars like right fielder Ken Griffey, shortstop Davey Concepcion, and center fielder Cesar Geronimo also played every day. It was a line-up without a weak spot. The team had speed and power. They hit 124 homers and stole 168 bases. They scored 840 runs, 105 more than the team with the second highest total. Their defense was superb, as evidenced by the fact that four Reds—Concepcion, Bench, Morgan, and Geronimo—all won Gold Gloves for being the best fielder at their position.

The Reds' pitching was made up of three solid starters and a very strong bullpen. Manager George "Sparky" Anderson earned the additional nickname of "Captain Hook" that season for the quick way he removed pitchers. The Reds once went 45 consecutive games without a complete pitching performance. Anderson could do much maneuvering with his pitching because he had relievers like Rawley Eastwick, Will McEnaney, Clay Carroll, Clay Kirby, and Fred Norman.

The Boston Red Sox were also an interesting team. They were making their first post-season appearance since 1967, when they lost the World Series in seven games to the St. Louis Cardinals. As a team, the Sox were quite the opposite of the Reds. For the most part, they were a young team. Before the season started, most people had little regard for them or their pennant chances. They had a great 36-year-old veteran in Carl Yastrzemski, but who would play shortstop, left field, and center? Would catcher Carlton Fisk bounce back from his injuries and play as he did before? And what about the pitching staff? Did the Red Sox have any pitchers who were both good and healthy?

All the questions were answered to the satisfaction of any Red Sox fan during the season. Fisk got healthy and once again was the best catcher in the American League. Rick Burleson came up from the minor leagues and played shortstop so well that he became the team's one indispensable player. Dwight Evans, who had been so tentative in right field, took charge and became a strong defensive force as well as somebody who could be counted on with a bat. Right-handed pitcher Rick Wise's arm got healthy and, along with Luis Tiant, Rogelio Moret and Bill Lee, gave manager Darrell Johnson a respectable starting rotation.

The key players to lead the Red Sox resurgence, however, were none of the above. The team's upward mobility revolved around two rookie outfielders, left fielder Jim Rice and center fielder Fred Lynn. They may have been the most memorable and effective rookie outfield duet in history.

Lynn very simply turned the American League upside down. He became the first player in league history to be named both Rookie of the Year and Most Valuable Player. He batted .331, with 21 homers, 105 r.b.i.'s and a league-leading 103 runs scored. The 23-year-old from the University of Southern California was a top major leaguer from the moment he stepped on a ball field.

Jim Rice was a basher, a huge raw talent whom people correctly saw as one of the great right-handed power hitters of the future. Even though he missed the month of September because of a broken arm, he still managed to hit 25 homers, drive in 102 runs and score 92, while batting .309. Who knows what the outcome of the Series would have been if he had been available?

The Bosox made short work of the Oakland A's in the divisional play-offs. They swept the three-time World Champions, winning each of the three games easily. The Sox were ready.

They proved how ready they were when they beat Cincinnati 6–0 in the first game, behind the immaculate pitching of Luis Tiant. The game was played in Boston's old Fenway Park, with its famous short, but high, left-field wall, dubbed the "Green Monster." Fenway gave the game a decided and delicious old-time baseball flavor. Tiant took that flavor and made it into his personal recipe. He completely stifled the Reds.

Though the first game's score was 6–0, it was far from a one-sided affair. The game had been scoreless for the first six-and-a-half innings. Cincinnati's young Don Gullett, who had a 15–4 record, was matching

Tiant pitch for pitch. The goose eggs ended in the last of the seventh. It was Tiant himself who keyed the rally. The pitcher led the inning off with a single, and by the time he made the third out, six runs had scored. The underdog Bostonians had won four straight games in 1975 post-season play. Any thoughts the Reds had of going right through them had been proven wrong.

The second game was played in a steady drizzle. Because of the huge Sunday-afternoon television audience, the game was played. In the seventh inning, a hard downpour held the contest up for 27 minutes. Between the raindrops, they managed to get a very wet game in.

Boston, with Bill Lee on the mound, carried a 2–1 lead into the ninth. Johnny Bench doubled to right to open the frame. Manager Darrell Johnson, wasting no time, replaced Lee with right-hander Dick Drago. Drago got Tony Perez to bounce to shortstop Rick Burleson, who made a good play near second base, throwing Perez out. Bench moved to third. Then Drago, working very carefully, got the dangerous George Foster to fly out to Yastrzemski in short left field, Bench holding at third. Drago had almost escaped unscathed when Concepcion beat out a slow bouncer over second to score the tying run. He then stole second and scored on Griffey's double to the left center-field wall. A game the Red Sox thought they had went to the Reds.

The third game was played at Cincinnati's new Riverfront Stadium. A record-tying six home runs left the premises that day, but a controversial call on a bunt in the tenth inning helped decide the outcome.

The Bosox, down 5–1 at one point, fought back and eventually tied the score at 5–5. A dramatic two-run homer by Dwight Evans in the top of the ninth knotted the game and set the stage for a hectic tenth.

Center fielder Cesar Geronimo led off the inning with a single to center. Pinch hitter Ed Armbrister, attempting to sacrifice the runner to second, laid down a bunt. The ball bounced just a few feet in front of the plate and Carlton Fisk went to field it. There was a momentary collision between Armbrister and Fisk before the catcher picked up the ball and threw it wildly into center field, attempting a force play. Because of the wild peg, the Reds had second and third and no out, and the umpires had a group of mad, swarming Red Sox screaming at them. The Sox claimed interference. The plate umpire refuted the Red Sox claim.

A few minutes later, with the bases loaded and one out, Joe Morgan slammed a drive over Fred Lynn's head for the game-winning hit. The game was history—Reds 6, Red Sox 5.

The Red Sox went back to Luis Tiant in Game Four, and again the Cuban right hander won, 5–4. Though his pitching was not quite as artistic this time, his heart and guts pulled him through. Despite being in trouble early, and giving up nine hits and four walks, Tiant shut the Reds out after the fourth inning, preserving the Boston win.

In Game Five, Tony Perez, a key member of Cincinnati's Big Red Machine, broke out of an 0-for-15 hitting slump, cracking two homers, and Don Gullett pitched a fine ball game as the Reds won 6–2. After five games, the Reds led three games to two.

Game Six was not played for four days. Only one off day was scheduled. The other three were caused by rainstorms which swept the New England coast. In a way, it was poetic that the sixth game be set off from the other five, as exciting as they were. The sixth game of the 1975 shindig was one of the most thrilling moments in World Series history. It deserved a stage of its own.

Freddy Lynn put Boston in front in the home half of the first with a three-run homer off Reds' starter Gary Nolan. Gloom filled the Cincinnati dugout. They had spotted three runs to Luis Tiant, a very unhealthful proposition.

For four innings, the Reds did nothing against Tiant. But suddenly in the fifth, with one man out, the situation changed dramatically. Ed Armbrister, pinch-hitting for the Reds' third pitcher of the game, Jack Billingham, walked. Pete Rose singled Armbrister to third. Both scored when Ken Griffey drove a triple off the wall in deep center field. Lynn, a superb fielder, jumped for the ball, missed it, but didn't miss the wall. He banged into it at full speed and collapsed in a heap. Luckily, he was only momentarily stunned, and stayed in the game. Johnny Bench then pulled a ball off the left-field wall, the first Red to hit the vaunted "Green Monster," and the score was tied as Griffey trotted in from third.

In the seventh and eighth innings, Cincinnati caught up with the 35-year-old right-hander. Griffey and Morgan both singled and both scored on a two-out double by George Foster. In the eighth, Geronimo led off with a home run pulled down the right-field line. That was all for Tiant and, apparently, for the Red Sox.

But the Bosox were a resilient team. Lynn led off the Boston eighth with a single off the leg of the sixth Cincinnati hurler, Pedro Borbon. After third baseman Rico Petrocelli walked, Rawley Eastwick came in, Anderson's seventh pitcher. When Eastwick fanned Dwight Evans and got Rick Burleson on an easy fly ball, it seemed as if Mr. Anderson could end his shuttle from the bullpen. But then pinch hitter Bernie Carbo, who had once played for the Reds, came up and kept his old team in the World Series. Batting for pitcher Rogelio Moret, who had replaced Tiant, he slammed a two-strike pitch into the center-field bleachers for a three-run homer, tying the score.

The Red Sox were charging now. In the last half of the ninth inning, they went for the kill. They loaded the bases with no one out. Then Lynn hit a looping drive down the left-field line. At first, it looked as if it would fall in, but George Foster, ignoring the danger of the wall that ran parallel to the foul line, charged over and caught the ball right on the line. He then wheeled and threw a perfect strike to the plate. The ball and runner Denny Doyle arrived almost at the same time and when the dust had cleared, Doyle was out and a great double play had kept the Reds alive.

In the top of the 11th, it was Boston's turn to hold the National League champions off. Leadoff hitter Pete Rose was hit by a pitch, but he was out at second when Fisk grabbed Griffey's sacrifice bunt attempt and fired him out. Morgan then hit a drive that seemed destined for the right-field seats. But Dwight Evans ran back to the wall, leaped, and made a remarkable catch. In one motion, he turned to the

A happy Carlton Fisk celebrates his game-winning homer. (1975)

infield and threw the ball to first base. Ken Griffey was doubled off first by plenty.

In the top of the 12th, Cincinnati was at it again. They threatened and came right on the verge of scoring, but were held off. In the bottom of the 12th, Carlton Fisk led off. At 12:34 A.M., after taking the first pitch for a ball, he tagged a long drive toward the "Green Monster." The ball kept drifting toward foul territory as it headed out into the night. As he made his way toward first slowly, Fisk was emphatic in his body language. He moved every which way trying to coax the ball to stay fair. When it finally cleared the wall in fair territory for a game-winning homer, Fisk jumped straight up into the air, as did everyone else in Boston.

If possible, the seventh game seemed anti-climactic. Nothing could top yesterday. But Game Seven, not willing to take a back seat to yesterday's game, was also a high-class thriller. In the ninth inning, the score was tied, 3–3. Griffey led off by walking. He was sacrificed to second and went to third on a ground out. With two out, Joe Morgan tapped a shallow fly to center and, when it fell in, the Reds took a lead they held. A great Cincinnati team had won the first of its two consecutive championships. A gallant Boston team came as close as possible before succumbing. Baseball, the sport that had been shoved into the national shadows by football over the past few years, rose up and showed that it was still the nation's number-one sport with a World Series that wowed them in every section of the country.

REGGIE JACKSON
HITS THREE HOME RUNS
IN ONE GAME—1977

Once again in 1977, the Series participants were the Yankees and Dodgers. For the second time, it was a cross-country meeting. The Brooklyn Dodgers were no more. In 1977, as in 1963, the Dodgers versus the Yankees meant Los Angeles against New York. In 1963, for the second time in their eight struggles with the Yankees, the Dodgers prevailed. That year, behind the airtight pitching of Sandy Koufax and Don Drysdale, the Dodgers swept the Yankees in four straight games.

Soon after their 1963 summit meeting, both franchises fell on bad times. In the late 1960s, the Dodgers were second-division occupants on a regular basis. It wasn't until the early 1970s that they regained their contender status.

The Yankees' tailspin was more pronounced. Two years after they lost the seventh game of the World Series to St. Louis, they fell to last place in the American League. For more than a decade, they were just another team. From 1964 until 1976, they failed to win a pennant. Most of that time, they ended the season in the American League's lower depths.

New York's troubles weren't just on the playing field. They had changed ownership twice during their bad years. The Dan Topping-Del Webb partnership that had owned the Yankees since the end of World War II sold the team to CBS Television in 1964. Ten years of poor performances and declining attendance convinced the network to sell the team to the present ownership, a group of businessmen of which George Steinbrenner is the principal partner. Steinbrenner, an aggressive man, tried to push the Yankees back to the top quickly, but it was difficult. Teams like Baltimore, Detroit, and Boston had a large edge in talent. It seemed likely under the rules of baseball in 1973 that it would take some time for New York to get back to respectability. But two legal decisions, one in 1974, the other in 1975, speeded up the process greatly.

After the 1974 season, Oakland's great pitcher, Jim "Catfish" Hunter, became involved in a contract dispute with Charles O. Finley, the Oakland owner. Their argument was taken to an arbitrator who ruled in Hunter's favor. Suddenly, a great pitcher was a free agent, legally allowed to sign with anybody. Steinbrenner signed Hunter, and the Yankees' restructuring was under way.

The 1975 decision was even more far reaching. This time, an arbitrator ruled that baseball's reserve clause, which bound a player to a club for his entire life, was illegal. A player was a free agent, the arbitrator said, once his contract was up. That meant that every player in baseball at one time or another could become a free agent. In the next few years, several top players played out their contract with one team, then signed with another as a free agent. Suddenly, an owner with a lot of money could build a good team quickly if he invested wisely in the free-agent market. Steinbrenner invested wisely.

Going into the 1977 season, the Yankees, the defending American League champions, bolstered their team when they signed Cincinnati's star left-handed pitcher, Don Gullett, as a free agent. That year, Gullett won 14 and lost 4, adding a strong arm to the New York starting corps.

New York also signed Reginald Martinez Jackson as a free agent for the 1977 season. Jackson was a vital force on an Oakland team that won five straight divisional titles (1971–1975) and three straight World Championships (1972–1974). Prior to his signing with the Yankees, Jackson had spent nine years in the majors and developed into one of the leading power hitters of his era.

Jackson was not only a unique performer on the field, he was also a controversial personality. Wherever he went, he seemed to attract attention, supporters, and critics. He signed a five-year, three-million dollar contract with George Steinbrenner to play in New York, but that was only a beginning. In New York, his name went up in lights. A candy bar was named after him. He was on television and in major magazines all the time. Books were written about him. He became one of America's biggest celebrities. His performance in the sixth game of the 1977 World Series, one of the most thrilling moments in World Series history, was a major factor in making Reggie Jackson a household name.

Swinging Reggie Jackson socks his second of three home runs. (1978)

The Dodgers came into the 1977 Series confident that they would hand the Yankees their second straight Series defeat. Unlike New York, their team had been built in the old-fashioned way. Primarily, the Dodgers were a group of farm-system products. If a position needed strengthening and a youngster wasn't available, then the team moved into the trading mart. The Dodgers shunned free agents. They felt their system had kept them competitive, and they weren't about to change. They were sure that only a team as good as the 1975–76 Reds could have beaten them out. Now the Reds were in disrepair. Don Gullett had defected to the Yankees, and Tony Perez had been traded away. The Dodgers stepped into the vacuum and became 1977's National League Champs.

The Dodgers had power, speed, and pitching. Four players—first baseman Steve Garvey, third baseman Ron Cey, left fielder Dusty Baker, and right fielder Reggie Smith—had all hit 30 or more homers. Second baseman Davey Lopes had stolen 47 bases to lead a team that stole 114. They had a five-man pitching rotation that included Tommy John, who had won 20, Rick Rhoden, who had won 16, Don Sutton and Doug Rau, who had each won 14, and Burt Hooten, who had put 12 in the win column.

Both teams were ready for action. The first game of the 1977 Series was played at Yankee Stadium. The New York starter was free-agent Don Gullett. Manager Billy Martin's choice of Gullett was a surprise because the left-hander had been having shoulder problems for the last month of the season. He had pitched only two innings in the play-offs. Gullett's mound opponent was the veteran right-hander, Don Sutton.

Martin's gamble seemed disasterous at the start. Los Angeles scored two runs in the first inning and Gullett seemed on the verge of a quick departure. But he took command and held the Dodgers scoreless until the ninth. In the meantime, the Yankees scored single runs in the first, sixth, and eighth. They came into the ninth leading 3–2. In the top of the ninth, Gullett ran out of strength, and the Dodgers pushed over the tying run. The game went into the 12th. In the Dodger half of each of the extra innings, they went out one, two, three. The Yankees put men on in each inning, but failed to cash them in. In the last of the 12th, however, a double, a walk, and a single gave the Yankees a win.

The second game was played on October 12. Martin again tried to get past the Dodgers with a sore-armed pitcher. Catfish Hunter, who hadn't pitched since September 10 because of arm problems, was lathered by the Dodger bats. The Dodgers won easily, 6–1, with Burt Hooten the recipient of their healthy attack.

In Los Angeles for Game Three, the Yankees finally started a healthy pitcher. Big right-hander Mike Torres was Martin's choice. His opponent was 20-game winner Tommy John. New York jumped on John for three runs and four hits in their first at bat. That lead held up till the third frame. That's when Dusty Baker belted a three-run homer to tie the game up. The cheering had barely subsided when the Yankees got the lead again. They pushed single runs across in the fourth and fifth innings and won the game 5–3, as Mike Torres got stronger as the game progressed. After three games, the Yankees led, two games to one.

Game Four was a pivotal game for the Dodgers. They couldn't lose and realistically expect to win the World Series. Even though it was a "must" game, Dodger manager Tommy Lasorda gambled with his pitching selection. This time, he chose the hurler with an ailing wing, left-hander Doug Rau. Rau had been 11–1 at the All-Star break, but had done little pitching since. The Yankees knocked Rau out of the box before he could retire a batter in the second inning. In that frame, the Yankees scored three runs. The Yankees coasted to a 4–2 victory behind the powerful pitching of young Ron Guidry. Guidry had been New York's best pitcher during the second half of the season. Except for a mistake to Davey Lopes, who hit Guidry's pitch for a two-run homer, the lefty from Louisiana handled the Dodgers flawlessly. He gave up only four hits, walked three, and struck out seven.

A portent of things to come came about in the top of the sixth. That's when Reggie Jackson hit his first homer of the Series.

Martin tried to win the Series in the enemy's home park with Don Gullett. Los Angeles would have none of that. They belted the left-hander for eight hits and seven runs in less than five innings. They led 10–0 after six and the four Yankee runs came after the contest was decided. For the second straight day, Reggie Jackson hit a homer. This day he did it on his last at bat.

Game Six was back at Yankee Stadium, sometimes called "The Bronx Zoo." Once again, a full house was on hand—56,000 people in for the kill. On a cool night, with overcoats and hot chocolate the motif, the Dodgers scored first. The two runs they got off Mike Torres were unearned. Yankee shortstop Bucky Dent was Los Angeles' unwilling benefactor. With two out, he dropped Reggie Smith's ground ball. Then Ron Cey walked and Steve Garvey drove them both home by slapping an outside pitch into the right-field corner for a triple. Reggie Jackson got over to the ball quickly, but then bobbled the ball ever so slightly. No error was charged.

Over his career, Jackson had always looked more comfortable with a bat in his hand rather than with a glove on it. In the last of the second, he walked on four successive balls. When first baseman Chris Chambliss followed with a long homer off Dodger starter Burt Hooten, the score was tied. In the top of the third, Reggie Smith rode a ball out of the park, his third four-bagger of the Series. The Dodgers went ahead 3–2. It would be their last lead.

Los Angeles appeared to have a rally going in the fourth, but shoddy base running took them out of the inning. Center fielder Rick Monday plunked a broken-bat pop fly into center field for a single. Catcher Steve Yeager pulled a ball into the left-field corner for what looked like a sure double. But Yeager hesitated rounding first, and when he finally decided to try for second, it was too late. Yankee left fielder Lou Pinella easily shot him down with a good throw and a rally went by the boards.

The Yankees didn't help Hooten with poor base running in their half of the inning. In fact, this was the inning they sent Hooten to an early shower. Catcher Thurman Munson, who had a hit in each game of this Series, led off with a single. Then Reggie Jackson, with the World Series spotlight on him, hit Hooten's first pitch for a homer and the Yankees led 4–3. Chambliss followed with a double, and he eventually scored so that, at the end of four, the Yanks led 5–3.

Elias Sosa was pitching when Jackson came to the plate in the last of the fifth. There were two out and a runner on first. Once again, number 44 picked on the first pitch and sent it out of sight. The Yankees now led 7–3, and there was hardly a dry eye in Los Angeles. It was becoming increasingly evident that the World Series would end tonight in New York's favor.

Nothing that happened between the fifth and eighth innings gave anyone any reason to think differently. Mike Torres was holding the Dodgers off easily. In those three innings, they got exactly one base runner on, and he was erased by a double play.

In the last of the eighth, the noise in Yankee Stadium was deafening. People couldn't hear the jets overhead, the noise was so loud. Charley

Hough, the fourth Dodger pitcher, was beginning his second inning of work. A knuckleball specialist, Hough knew better than to try anything but his best pitch against the leadoff batter, Reggie Jackson. Jackson was smoking, on fire at the plate. When he moved out of the on-deck circle, he was greeted with a thunderous ovation. Hough pitched a knuckleball that didn't knuckle and Jackson sent the ball into orbit. It finally came down 450 feet from the plate, in the center-field bleachers. Jackson didn't move from the plate until the ball started to descend. He admired the majestic flight of the ball as much as the fans did. He finally made his way around the bases to overwhelming applause. It was one of the most thrilling moments in World Series history. As if on cue, Reggie Jackson, "Mr. October," who made a habit of getting big hits in important games, had done it again.

The Series ended with an 8–4 Yankee victory. After the Dodgers scored a meaningless run in the ninth, the record keepers took over. They spelled out Jackson's Series statistics in marvelous detail. In Game Six, he had three homers in three consecutive at bats. Only Babe Ruth had hit three homers in a Series game before, but he hadn't done it in consecutive times at bat.

Jackson drove in five runs that night. He scored four times to tie a record. Jackson had hit a homer on his last trip to the plate in Game Five. Each homer in Game Six was hit on the first pitch. Thus he had hit four homers on four consecutive swings.

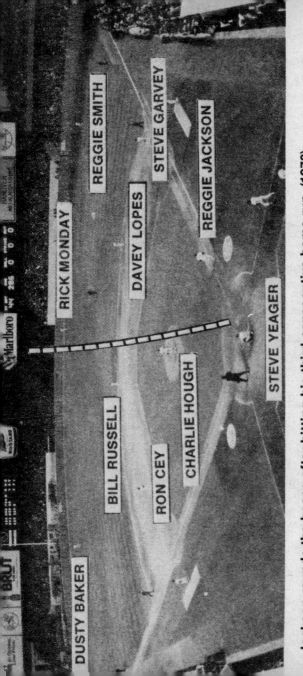

DUSTY BAKER · BILL RUSSELL · RON CEY · CHARLIE HOUGH · STEVE YEAGER · RICK MONDAY · REGGIE SMITH · DAVEY LOPES · STEVE GARVEY · REGGIE JACKSON

Jackson rounds the bases after hitting his third consecutive home run. (1978)

He was the first man to hit five homers in a Series. He scored 10 runs, the most ever. He had 25 total bases in the Series, the most ever. He tied a record with 12 total bases in the sixth game. He batted .450 for the Series.

Before this Series, people would tease Reggie by calling him "Mr. October." Though they would say it dripping with sarcasm, Reggie liked the name. He liked its sound, and what it meant. He thought it emphasized that he was the number-one man when the games were all-important. In the 1977 World Series, Reggie Jackson proved he was worthy of that nickname.